THE POWER OF GUEST PODCASTING

The Power of Guest Podcasting:
How to Get Booked, Build Authority, and Grow Your Business

Publisher: Rose Avenue Press

Los Angeles, California

This is a work of nonfiction intended for educational and informational purposes only. The author has made every effort to ensure the accuracy of the information contained in this book, but assumes no responsibility for errors or omissions. Some examples have been simplified or anonymized to protect privacy and improve clarity.

Results described in this book are not guaranteed. Individual outcomes will vary based on effort, experience, market conditions, and other factors beyond the author's control. The author is not liable for any losses, damages, or other liabilities that may arise from the use of this book.

Library of Congress Control Number: 2026900369

ISBN: 9798994493502 (paperback)
ISBN: 9798994493519 (hardback)
ISBN: 9798994493526 (ebook)
ISBN: 9798994493533 (audiobook)

First Edition: 2026

Printed in the United States of America

THE POWER OF GUEST PODCASTING

HOW TO GET BOOKED, BUILD AUTHORITY, AND GROW YOUR BUSINESS

BRANDON LEIBOWITZ

To Lini

FOREWORD BY ALEX SANFILIPPO

I first met Brandon Leibowitz in 2021 through my podcast host/guest matching platform, PodMatch. I was looking for guests for my show, and he was looking to be a guest. His profile and experience really stuck out to me. I could tell he was experienced, so I took an extra step and connected with Brandon on LinkedIn as well. I knew he was the type of person I wanted to be connected with and to learn from.

Since meeting Brandon, I've watched him go from a new podcast guest to becoming an in-demand, ideal guest sought out by many podcast hosts on PodMatch and off the platform. I've seen Brandon's name pop up on a lot of podcasts I listen to. It's been amazing to see!

I bring all of this up to say that I am really excited that Brandon is (finally) publishing a book on the topic of podcast guesting, using his approach, which, clearly works incredibly well!

I never write a foreword to a book that I don't read first, so I went through this book. And as a highly experienced podcast guest (and host) myself, I can say with confidence that this is a complete guide from start to finish on how to become a successful podcast guest that hosts and listeners will love.

Brandon, thank you for putting this together and not keeping your wisdom and secret sauce to yourself! Thank you for helping make podcasting a better place by training future guests to be as impactful as you are!

Now, to you, the reader, get a pen and a highlighter ready, you're going to learn a lot from Brandon really fast. My advice is this, implement in real time, keep guesting even while you're learning. Guidance + practice is a winning formula. I'm excited to hear you as a guest on some podcasts!

— Alex Sanfilippo
Founder of PodMatch
podmatch.com

ACKNOWLEDGMENTS

This book exists because of the podcast hosts who opened their microphones and trusted me with their audiences. Thank you for the conversations, the curiosity, and the opportunities. Every interview helped shape the system you are about to read.

I am grateful to the marketers, founders, coaches, and business owners who tested these strategies in the real world. Your results, questions, and feedback helped refine what works and what does not.

Thank you to the friends, collaborators, and mentors who pushed me to document this process rather than keep it in my head. You reminded me that systems only create leverage when they are shared.

Most of all, thank you to the readers who are willing to raise their hand, tell their story, and show up consistently. Guest podcasting rewards action. If this book helps you take that next step, then it has done its job.

Thank you to my fiancée, Lini, for the constant support, patience, and encouragement that made this book possible.

PREFACE

I remember when I first thought about starting my own podcast in 2020. I had no idea where to begin. The world had just shut down, and like many others, I felt lost.

Before that, I regularly taught in person digital marketing classes at General Assembly, SCORE, and the Small Business Administration. I also hosted my own seminars and Meetup events. These workshops consistently generated new clients for my digital marketing agency.

Each month, I taught sessions covering search engine optimization, Google Ads, social media marketing, and other core digital marketing topics. It worked well.

Until it didn't. When everything shut down, that entire pipeline disappeared almost overnight.

With one of my main lead generation channels gone, I had to pivot quickly. I decided to start my own podcast focused on digital marketing strategies. I had zero experience with podcasting beyond listening to a few random episodes here and there.

I turned to Google, Reddit, and online forums to figure it out. After a lot of trial and error, more error than I like to admit, I eventually built a system that worked.

I kept my podcast active for about a year and a half. It was fun, fulfilling, and opened the door to new opportunities. But over time, I discovered something unexpected.

I was getting more value from being a guest on other people's podcasts than from hosting my own.

It started with an email invitation to be a guest on someone else's show. The idea immediately intrigued me. With my background in SEO, I recognized the power of tapping into an existing audience that already trusted the host.

It was a clear win-win. I shared my knowledge while benefiting from their reach and credibility.

That first guest appearance did not go smoothly.

I had microphone issues. The host had connection problems. The recording ultimately had to be rescheduled.

But that moment marked the beginning of something much bigger.

Since then, I have refined guest podcasting into a repeatable system. I learned how to find the right shows, get booked, deliver value during interviews, and maximize each appearance long after the episode goes live.

That failed recording turned out to be the foundation of a strategy that continues to transform my business.

No more worrying about scripts, editing, or building an audience from scratch. The host handles the production.

I simply show up, share insights, and build authority. All while saving time and money.

Guest podcasting was not just easier. It was smarter.

I am not suggesting you abandon your own podcast if you already have one. But I do believe every expert, entrepreneur, or service provider gains real value by exploring the power of being a guest on other shows. The ROI is clear and profitable.

Guest podcasting allows you to establish yourself as a subject matter expert and increase your visibility with targeted audiences.

It creates meaningful networking opportunities and gives you a natural way to promote your products or services without sounding salesy.

It also boosts your SEO, sharpens your communication skills, and helps you generate evergreen content that keeps working long after the interview ends.

All with little to no cost beyond your time.

Anyone can replicate this strategy if they follow the right process. Your success is not out of reach. It is closer than you think. That is what this book is about. Let's dive in.

CONTENTS

INTRODUCTION

I did not set out to become a podcast guest, but showing up on the right shows changed my business faster than anything else I tried.

"Marketing is no longer about the stuff you make, but the stories you tell."
— Seth Godin

Podcasting has exploded over the past decade. Not just in size, but in influence. With nearly 500 million monthly listeners globally and growing at over 10 % per year, podcasting has become one of the most trusted and personal forms of media. People listen while commuting, working, exercising, or relaxing.

But most importantly, they listen attentively. Unlike fast scrolling on social media or skipping YouTube ads, podcast listeners engage with content for 20, 40, even 60 minutes or more at a time. That makes podcasts one of the most powerful ways to reach a highly focused, deeply loyal audience.

But here is the shift most people miss. You do not need your own podcast to benefit. In fact, being a guest on other people's podcasts can be more effective than running your own.

Guest podcasting gives you something incredibly valuable: access. You are borrowing the trust, reach, and platform that someone else has already built. You do not need to grow your own show from scratch, manage episodes, or edit audio or video. You simply show up, share your story, deliver value, and tap into a warm, ready made audience.

That is how I grew my digital marketing agency, SEO Optimizers. I started out just trying to stay visible during the pandemic, at a time when traditional marketing felt uncertain and expensive. Through guest podcasting, I found something even better than visibility. I found growth, credibility, and leads.

Appearing on hundreds of podcasts over the years has led to new clients, high authority backlinks, media features, speaker invitations, improved SEO rankings, and a long lasting digital footprint. All of this required far less time and effort than hosting my own show.

What You Will Learn

This book is a step by step system for getting booked on podcasts that actually move your business forward. The shows your audience is already listening to and trusting.

You will learn how to:

- Identify relevant, high quality podcasts in your niche
- Find accurate contact information for podcast hosts
- Write a compelling pitch that gets you booked
- Prepare for podcast interviews with confidence
- Deliver value in a way that builds trust and converts listeners
- Promote your episodes to create long-term brand exposure
- Avoid common mistakes that limit visibility and opportunities

This book is designed to make guest podcasting accessible, repeatable, and effective. Even if you are just getting started, these strategies will help you show up confidently, get booked consistently, and turn interviews into real business growth.

Who This Book Is For

If you have a story to share, expertise to offer, or a brand to build, this book is for you.

Guest podcasting is an ideal strategy for:

- Business owners and entrepreneurs who want to attract ideal clients and build lasting authority
- Coaches, authors, and consultants ready to scale visibility and credibility
- Marketers and SEO professionals focused on earning high authority backlinks and brand exposure
- Creators and thought leaders who want to connect more deeply with their audience through voice

You do not need to be a natural speaker to succeed. I will walk you through how to prepare, show up confidently, and follow up after each interview so you can perform like a seasoned pro.

Why Guest Podcasting Works So Well

There are many marketing channels available today, including social media, email, SEO, video, and blogging, but podcasting works differently. It builds deeper, longer lasting connections. When people hear your voice and watch you speak, they feel like they know you. That familiarity leads to trust, curiosity, and action. Listeners look you up, follow up, and often convert.

Beyond the human connection, guest podcasting delivers powerful technical benefits. Many podcasts are published on websites that provide high authority, niche relevant backlinks. Every appearance has the potential to strengthen your SEO, increase organic visibility, and drive long-term traffic back to your site.

In a world where attention is fragmented and trust is increasingly difficult to earn, podcasting addresses both. When you show up as a guest on the right shows, you are not just sharing information. You are borrowing credibility, building authority, and positioning yourself as someone worth listening to.

How to Use This Book

This book walks you through the entire process of becoming a consistent and effective podcast guest. Each chapter builds on the last, so I recommend reading in order, especially if you are new to guest podcasting.

Along the way, you will find practical guidance, real world insights, and proven strategies to help you get booked faster, speak with confidence, and make each appearance count.

Throughout the book, you will see callouts for SEO tips, common mistakes to avoid, and promotion checklists designed to help you extract more value from every interview. Everything here is based on what I have tested and used successfully for myself and my clients.

By the end of this book, you will have the systems and confidence to appear on one podcast a week or more and turn those appearances into measurable growth for your business or personal brand. This is not an overnight growth hack. But when applied consistently, the results compound long after the interview ends.

How to Use the Bonus Resources in This Book

Each chapter includes a bonus resource section to help you apply what you just learned. These resources include templates, checklists, examples, and frameworks that remove guesswork and save you time. Instead of building everything from scratch, you can start with tools that are already proven.

All bonus resources live in one place so you can access them anytime. Simply visit **seooptimizers.com/bonus**

From there, select the resource that matches the chapter you are working through and download it when you need it. Whether you read cover to cover or jump between chapters, the resources are organized to support both approaches.

For best results, focus on one chapter at a time and use the corresponding bonus resource before moving on. Action is where momentum builds, and small steps taken consistently lead to lasting growth.

Let's Get You Booked

You do not need a massive following, a bestselling book, or a big PR team to succeed with podcast guesting. With a clear strategy, a compelling story, and a repeatable process, you can start landing interviews that build your brand, authority, and long-term visibility.

The approach works. Let's get started.

PART 1

THE SETUP
(GETTING THE YES)

FINDING PODCASTS THAT ACTUALLY MOVE THE NEEDLE

Discover podcasts that help you reach the right audience, build lasting authority, and create meaningful business growth.

"Don't count the people you reach. Reach the people who count."
— David Ogilvy

The first step to success with guest podcasting is focus. You do not need to be everywhere. You just need to be in the right places. That means targeting shows that are active, have loyal listeners, and speak directly to your target audience.

Think about who you are trying to reach. Where do they spend time? What content do they trust? Which podcasts do they already subscribe to? That is where you need to be.

When I first started, I said yes to every podcast invite. I figured more was better. I quickly realized that being more selective delivered better results.

You do not want to waste your time on shows with no real audience or podcasts that do not align with your brand. This is especially true for brand-new podcasts, where it is often too soon to know who is listening or whether the show will stay active long-term.

The Hidden SEO Power of Podcast Guesting

After being on hundreds of podcasts, I have learned to prioritize shows that have both an engaged audience and a website. Why the website matters is simple. When your interview is published on a podcast's site with a link back to your website, it creates a backlink. And backlinks are gold for SEO.

Search engines, including Google and AI-driven systems, use links as trust signals. Every time a relevant site in your niche links to you, it is treated as a vote of credibility.

I saw this firsthand after appearing on a niche marketing podcast that published full show notes on their website. The episode itself did not drive a flood of traffic overnight, but the link back to my site was indexed within days.

A few weeks later, pages on my website started ranking for competitive keywords I had been stuck on for months. That single appearance continued sending referral traffic and SEO value long after the interview ended. That is the compounding effect most people overlook.

If a podcast only publishes episodes on platforms like Spotify or Apple Podcasts, that is still great for exposure. However, it will not help your search rankings the way a contextual backlink from a niche website will.

In this chapter, I will show you how to find high-quality podcasts using advanced search operators. You will learn how to evaluate shows based on audience fit, visibility, and backlink potential. Do not worry. It is easier than it sounds, and the payoff can be significant.

How to Use Google Like a Podcast-Finding Machine

Google is more than the place you want your website to rank. It is also a powerful discovery tool. With the right search tactics, it can help you uncover podcast opportunities that others in your space are missing.

General keyword searches are a good place to start, but advanced search operators give you far more precision. They allow you to find highly targeted podcasts that closely match your niche and audience.

Before I started using search operators, I was getting acceptable results. Once I added these tactics, the quality of podcasts I found improved dramatically.

Here are three search operators I use consistently:

- inurl: searches for keywords in the website URL
- intitle: searches for keywords in the page title
- intext: searches for keywords within the page content

Let's break these down with real life examples.

Find Podcasts with the Right Keywords in the URL

This search filters websites that include your keyword directly in the URL.

For example, go to Google and type:

```
inurl:"podcast" entrepreneur
```

This returns websites with the word podcast in the URL and entrepreneur appearing somewhere on the page. I use keywords such as entrepreneur, marketing, or business because they closely align with my audience. To customize this for your industry, simply swap in your own keyword.

If you're a fitness coach, try:

```
inurl:"podcast" fitness
```

If you sell dog products, try:

```
inurl:"podcast" dogs
```

Stick to one or two word phrases. Longer searches tend to get too narrow and often return lower quality results. Focus on broad but relevant topics you can confidently speak about that connect directly to your expertise or niche.

Find Podcasts with Your Topics in the Page Title

This search targets websites that include your keyword directly in the page title.

Search this:

```
intitle:"podcast" entrepreneur
```

These results often include podcast landing pages or blog posts where your keyword appears in the title. This is usually a strong signal that the podcast is relevant to your audience.

Your keyword does not need to describe your exact job title. Instead, think like your audience. If you sell dog food, do not limit yourself to that phrase alone.

Try related topics such as:

- pets
- animal health
- nutrition
- dog wellness

Search engines reward relevance, not exact matches. Using related keywords helps you discover podcasts your audience already trusts and follows.

One of the biggest advantages of using intitle: is that the results stay relevant even several pages deep. Unlike general searches that quickly drift off topic, advanced search operators allow you to sift through focused results that remain within your niche.

Dig Deeper: Find Keywords in the Body Text

Last, intext: looks for keywords within the body content of a webpage.

intext:"podcast" entrepreneur

This is useful after you have already searched using inurl: or intitle: and want to go one level deeper. For example, if you are looking for a podcast related to opening a gardening store, search:

intext:"podcast" gardening

This returns results where those keywords appear anywhere on the page, including blog posts, show notes, guest interviews, and directory listings.

No matter your niche, these search operators can help you discover podcasts your audience is already listening to. Swap out the keyword entrepreneur with a topic that fits your expertise, then start building a list of shows that align with your goals.

Once you have a list of prospects, the next step is deciding which podcasts are actually worth your time. Not every opportunity deserves a pitch, and being selective is what turns guest podcasting into a strategy instead of a guessing game.

Why This Matters

Finding the right podcasts is the foundation of everything that follows. When you focus on relevance first, every pitch, interview, and promotion effort works harder. This step alone separates strategic guest podcasting from wasted effort.

Action Step: Create Your Podcast Prospect List

Before moving on, set aside 30 minutes and build your first podcast prospect list.

Using the search operators from this chapter, aim to find:

- Ten podcasts that align with your audience
- Five shows with an active website
- Three podcasts you are genuinely excited to appear on

Do not overthink this. This list does not need to be perfect. It just needs to exist. You will refine it as you go.

Finding the right podcasts is only the first step. A show can look promising on the surface and still fail to deliver real results once you dig deeper.

Before you spend time pitching, you need a way to separate podcasts that simply sound good from podcasts that actually support your goals. That means slowing down just enough to qualify each opportunity before you reach out.

In the next section, I will walk you through how to quickly and confidently qualify podcasts so every pitch you send is intentional, relevant, and worth your effort.

Bonus Resource: Podcast Prospecting Spreadsheet

If you want a faster way to organize your research, I created a free podcast prospecting spreadsheet to help you track shows, websites, keywords, and notes as you build your list.

Access it here:

seooptimizers.com/bonus

Or scan the QR code below for instant access.

HOW TO QUALIFY PODCASTS BEFORE YOU PITCH

One well chosen podcast can outperform dozens of appearances on the wrong shows.

"The essence of strategy is choosing what not to do."
— Michael Porter

After you've found potential shows using advanced search operators, it's time to decide which ones are actually worth your time. Qualifying podcasts upfront protects your time, energy, and motivation.

Start by opening the websites from the first few pages of your search results. After page three, results can become off topic, although not always. Keep exploring until the content clearly stops fitting your goals.

If the results look irrelevant from the start, adjust your keyword. Expect some trial and error. Once you find a keyword that delivers quality results, use variations such as synonyms, plurals, and closely related terms with your search operators to broaden your reach.

Why Being on the Right Show Matters More Than Quantity

The more relevant a show is to your industry, niche, and audience, the more impact it will have.

Start with the basics. Look at the podcast name, episode titles, cover art, and descriptions. Do they match the type of content your ideal audience already consumes?

Skim a few episodes or listen to short clips to get a feel for the tone and format. If it sounds like something your audience enjoys, it is likely a good fit.

Do not overthink it. If you are unsure after a few minutes of reviewing the site or sampling an episode, move on. At this stage, you are looking for alignment and fit, not a deep audit.

Make Every Podcast Appearance Count

Getting featured on a podcast takes time. You have to pitch the host, prepare your talking points, and show up ready to deliver a strong interview.

Focus on podcasts that offer a strong return on investment. A good rule of thumb is this. If a show ranks well in Google search results, it likely has solid SEO value and authority. Higher ranking sites usually demonstrate strong experience, expertise, authority, and trustworthiness, often referred to as E-E-A-T.

That is the type of podcast you want to appear on. One with credibility and an established audience. Aim for shows with a proven track record. If a podcast is still on its first or second episode, skip it for now.

Early on, I made the mistake of saying yes to a podcast simply because the host was enthusiastic and the topic sounded close enough. The interview went fine, but the episode never made it to a website, was rarely promoted, and produced no lasting traffic or leads. Around the same time, I appeared on a smaller but more established show with an active website and engaged audience. That single episode continued driving traffic and visibility months later. The difference was not the conversation. It was the qualification.

Use Data to Find High-Impact Shows

In marketing, key performance indicators, or KPIs, help you measure what is working and what is not. The same principle applies when evaluating podcasts.

Instead of guessing, look at data that shows whether a podcast is established, active, and capable of reaching your target audience.

Quick Metrics to Spot a Valuable Show

Some performance data is easily available and provides a quick sense of how a podcast is doing.

Look for:

- Total number of listens, downloads, or views
- Subscriber count
- Episode ratings and reviews

These metrics provide a quick snapshot of a podcast's reach and audience engagement.

Check a Podcast's Authority Before You Pitch

You can also assess a podcast's website authority using SEO tools such as Ahrefs, Moz, or SEMrush.

These tools can show:

- How many backlinks the site has
- Which websites link to them
- The site's authority score
- Keywords the podcast ranks for

If a podcast website attracts backlinks from trusted or relevant sites, that is a strong green flag. Being featured on their site can give your own website a valuable SEO boost, which goes beyond simply being heard on the episode.

If you do not use SEO tools yet, do not let that stop you. Basic signals like search rankings, backlinks mentioned on the site, or consistent publishing habits can still guide smart decisions.

Hidden Clues That Reveal a Podcast's Popularity

Not all performance data is public. Metrics like listener retention, location, or device type are usually only available to the host.

That said, you can still uncover valuable insight in other ways. Start by checking the podcast's social media presence.

Look for:

- Engagement such as likes, comments, and shares
- Milestones or listener count announcements
- Audience interaction with episodes or guest appearances

If a podcast recently celebrated one thousand downloads or consistently receives strong engagement, that is a clear signal the show is worth your attention.

Platforms like YouTube, Instagram, TikTok, Facebook, LinkedIn, and X (formerly Twitter) can offer additional clues about audience size and loyalty. A strong presence on even one platform is often a reliable indicator of an engaged audience.

You can also:

- Look for behind-the-scenes episodes where the host shares stats or growth updates
- Join the email newsletter, since hosts often share highlights, download milestones, or subscriber goals
- Listen to one or two recent episodes to evaluate production quality and audience interaction

By combining signals from multiple sources, you get a clearer picture of which podcasts are active, credible, and aligned with your goals.

Compare and Prioritize the Best Podcast Leads

Now that you have gathered podcast leads that are relevant and aligned with your expertise, it is time to separate the strongest opportunities from the rest.

From an SEO perspective, you are evaluating how much long-term value a podcast website can pass back to you.

Some of the most important podcast KPIs include:

- Total listens or views
- Subscriber count
- Total downloads
- Retention and average listening time
- Ratings and reviews
- Social media engagement, including shares, comments, and likes
- Audience growth rate
- Geographic reach

Popularity metrics only tell part of the story. SEO adds another layer to how valuable a podcast truly is over time.

From an SEO standpoint, these KPIs matter most. Look for:

- Relevancy of the podcast to your business
- Number of backlinks
- Keywords the podcast ranks for
- Authority score of the podcast website

Why Reach + Relevance = ROI

The more people who hear your message, the more likely some will take action. That action might be visiting your website, following you on social media, or engaging with your work.

This is why evaluating podcasts is such a critical part of guest podcasting. It helps you focus on shows that actually move the needle.

Guest podcasting offers powerful long-term benefits, but those benefits only compound when you choose the right shows. Everything starts with evaluating podcasts correctly so you can focus your effort on platforms that support real growth.

Why This Matters

Not every podcast deserves your time. The real leverage comes from choosing shows that align with your audience, your expertise, and your long-term goals. When you prioritize the right opportunities, every pitch becomes more focused and every appearance becomes more valuable.

Action Step: Narrow Your List to High Impact Shows

Take the podcast list you created in the previous chapter and narrow it down to your top five targets.

Use these filters:

- The show clearly speaks to your ideal audience
- The podcast has an active website
- The site shows signs of authority or visibility in search
- You can clearly imagine delivering real value to their listeners

These five podcasts will become your first outreach targets. This is where strategy replaces guesswork.

Finding podcasts is only the starting point. Not every show you uncover will be worth your time, energy, or attention. The real leverage comes from knowing which opportunities to pursue and which ones to skip.

In the next chapter, I will show you how to qualify podcasts before you pitch so every appearance has the potential to deliver real results.

Bonus Resource: Podcast Vetting Scorecard

To make this easier, I put together a podcast evaluation scorecard that walks you through relevance, reach, SEO value, and authority in one simple checklist. This is the same framework I use before pitching any show.
Access it here:
seooptimizers.com/bonus
Or scan the QR code below for instant access.

FINDING THE RIGHT CONTACT INFO WITHOUT WASTING HOURS

Finding the right contact matters more than sending more pitches, because even the best message fails in the wrong inbox.

"You can do everything right and still lose if you focus on the wrong priority."
— Stephen R. Covey

Now that you've got your list of podcasts you want to be on, the next step is actually getting in touch with someone who can say yes. Seems easy enough, right? Find an email, send a message. But this is where a lot of people get stuck. The truth is, if your message doesn't reach the right person, nothing else matters.

This chapter is about cutting through the noise and finding the best way to connect with the host or whoever is booking guests. You do not need to be a private investigator, and spending hours digging through the internet for a single email is a waste of time. I give myself fifteen minutes. If I cannot find a solid contact by then, I skip it.

Start by Finding the Right Person

A lot of podcasts are run by solo hosts. More often than not they're the one you want to contact. Some shows, especially larger ones, have producers or assistants who handle guest bookings. Your first job is to figure out who that person is.

If their website or podcast page doesn't make it obvious, try LinkedIn. Most hosts will mention their podcast in their profile, and if there's someone on their team who handles outreach, you'll probably find them there too. Job titles to look for include: producer, show coordinator, podcast manager. That's who you want to talk to.

Don't worry if you can't get directly to the host. Getting a response from the right team member can be just as good. They're often the ones making the call anyway.

Using Search Operators to Find Contact Information

If you know how to use Google the right way, you can find an email, contact page, or submission form in less than a few minutes. No cold-scrolling, just direct results.

We discussed search operators in the previous chapters, but here are more ways to use them. Let me walk you through exactly how I'd use them to find contact info for my own podcast, which is hosted by my agency, SEO Optimizers.

Start With Quotation Marks

When you're looking for a podcast contact info start by putting the podcast name in quotation marks. This tells Google you are searching for the exact phrase, not a loose match. Then just add the word contact.

For example:

```
"SEO Optimizers" contact
```

This simple search works better than most people expect. You can also replace the word contact with phrases such as guest submission or pitch.

Many podcasts have a dedicated page for guest inquiries. You just need to know what to look for. In many cases, this search will take you directly to a contact form, press page, or a public email address.

Use the Site: Operator to Focus Your Search

Let's say you know the website that hosts the podcast. Now you can tell Google to search only that site. Nothing else. By using the site: operator along with the word contact we get a specific search for the website's contact information.

Here's how it's done:

```
site:seooptimizers.com contact
```

This narrows the results quickly. Instead of scanning random listings, you are now focused only on pages from that specific domain.

Try Intext: When Things Get Tricky

If you still cannot find the contact page, use the intext: operator. This tells Google to search for a specific word within the actual content of a page. You can also combine it with the site: operator for even more precision.

Try this:

```
intext:contact site:seooptimizers.com
```

It is surprising how often this reveals hidden or unlabeled contact forms that do not show up otherwise.

Search the Website

Even the best search operators have limits. When that happens, it is time to explore the podcast's website directly.

Start by scrolling to the footer at the bottom of the site. Most contact information lives there. Look for pages labeled About, Contact, Advertising, Press, or Media. Do not skip the podcast page itself. Many shows list a guest submission link or host email there.

If none of these methods are getting you results, don't worry. It just means it's time to switch gears. When Google comes up empty and the site's a dead end, it's time to roll out phase two.

Other Methods to Find Contact Information

There are several ways to track down a podcast's contact information. Some are quicker than others. The search operators we covered are a strong starting point, but they will not work in every situation. When they come up short, it is time to broaden your approach.

Start with the podcast's social media profiles. Hosts often include contact details in their bio or link out to a guest submission form. If that does not work, explore podcast directories, review past guests, use email lookup tools, or tap into your existing network.

Finding Contact Info Through Social Media

Most podcasts today have some kind of social media presence. Whether it is Facebook, Instagram, YouTube, TikTok, LinkedIn, X, or Pinterest, chances are you will find at least one active profile connected to the show. That is often the easiest place to start making contact.

If you know the name of the podcast or the host, search for it directly on each platform. Many hosts list an email address or link to a guest submission form right in their bio. If you cannot find them on social media, check the podcast's website. Most sites link out to their social profiles in the footer, which gives you additional ways to connect.

Spread your search across multiple channels. The more places you check, the better your chances of finding the right person. Just avoid sending the same message everywhere. Tailor your outreach based on who you are contacting. We will cover exactly how to do that in the next chapter.

Here is an example from my own podcast, hosted by SEO Optimizers. If you visit our Facebook page, you will find our email and other contact information clearly listed. Many podcasts make this easy, especially those that are open to guests or advertisers. You just need to know where to look.

Even if an email address is not listed publicly, do not stop there. Most platforms allow you to send a direct message. I have landed interviews with major shows simply by sending a short, thoughtful DM. You never know who is checking the inbox. It may be the exact person you need to reach.

One pattern I have noticed is that messaging on X often works better than platforms like Instagram or TikTok. Smaller follower counts usually mean less noise, which makes your message harder to miss. Podcasts with smaller audiences can be great opportunities to build genuine, one on one connections.

I learned this firsthand with a podcast host I was unable to reach through their website or main social profiles. After trying several channels with no response, I discovered their personal X account. I sent a quick message, and they responded almost immediately, saying they loved the idea of having me on the show. Missing that profile meant missing the opportunity entirely.

At the end of the day, guest podcasting requires you to think like both an outreach specialist and a digital detective. The more platforms you explore and the more intentional your approach, the better your chances of connecting with the right host and landing guest spots that actually move the needle.

Using Podcast Directories to Get Discovered

Another smart way to find contact info and discover podcasts actively looking for guests is through podcast directories and matchmaking platforms. No, it's not what it sounds like. Let me explain.

Podcasts are shared on directories such as Apple Podcasts, Spotify, Amazon Music, and iHeartRadio. These platforms are great for browsing and discovering shows. You can filter by category, see who the host is, and even find contact details in the show description or linked website.

Beyond the major listening platforms are dedicated podcast networking sites built specifically to connect hosts with qualified guests. Sites such as PodMatch are designed for exactly what you're trying to do: get featured on podcasts. You create a profile, showcase your expertise, and start connecting with hosts who are actively searching for people like you. It's as simple as that.

These platforms don't just make discovery easier. They also let you filter by audience size, niche, format, and more. That means less guesswork and more targeted outreach.

And here's the bonus. Many of these directories give you a chance to boost your own visibility. By simply being on them, you're creating additional SEO value for yourself and opening the door to more inbound opportunities. Think of it as passive podcast pitching. Hosts can find you just as easily as you find them.

If you're serious about getting booked consistently, don't sleep on these websites. They're built for this exact purpose. They give you direct access to a pool of shows that are actively looking for guests.

Reaching Out to Former Podcast Guests

Sometimes the best way to connect with a podcast host is through someone who has already been a guest on the show.

If you take the time to listen to a few episodes, you will start to recognize the names of past guests. With a little research, you can usually find their website, social profiles, or email address. Introduce yourself, let them know you enjoyed their episode, and ask if they are open to sharing how they connected with the host.

This approach serves two purposes. First, it can lead to a warm introduction to the podcast you are targeting. Second, it opens the door to an entirely new network of podcasters and professionals who may be open to having you on their own shows. Many guest opportunities come from referrals, so one solid connection can go a long way.

I ran into this exact situation with a podcast host who did not respond no matter what I tried. I followed every step outlined in this book. I checked their website, searched social platforms, and sent multiple emails, but heard nothing back. Instead of giving up, I reviewed older episodes and tracked down past guests. I reached out to one of them, and they were kind enough to connect me directly with the host.

A few days later, the host replied and said they were excited to have me on. I mentioned that I had previously emailed them, and they told me they no longer monitored that inbox. Without reaching out to a former guest, I may have missed the opportunity entirely.

The takeaway is simple. Do not rely only on the most obvious contact methods. Someone who has already been a guest has successfully done what you are trying to do. Approach them politely, act professionally, and be clear about why the connection makes sense. One conversation can unlock opportunities you do not find any other way.

Using Email Hunter Tools

When other methods fall short, email hunter tools can help you uncover contact information that is not easily found through search or social media. When used responsibly, these tools can save time and help you reach the right decision makers behind a podcast.

One of the most widely used tools is Hunter.io. It is fast and straightforward. You enter a website or company name, and it returns a list of verified email addresses associated with that domain. Hunter uses a combination of data crawling and verification signals to reduce outdated or incorrect results.

I have used it to identify podcast hosts, producers, and marketing contacts in seconds. It is not a guaranteed solution, but it is a reliable backup when you have exhausted other options and need another way to move the conversation forward.

Tapping Into Your Personal Network

One of the easiest and most overlooked ways to land podcast interviews is not by Googling for hours or relying on tools. It is by reaching out to people already in your network.

If you have friends, past clients, or colleagues who have been guests on podcasts, or who host their own, start there. Send a quick message and ask if they are open to making an introduction or pointing you in the right direction. A warm intro from someone the host already trusts is far more effective than a cold pitch.

You can also ask friends and family what shows they listen to. Even if they are not in your industry, they may follow a niche podcast that aligns perfectly with your topic or story. This is a low effort way to discover opportunities you might never find through search alone.

Do not overlook mentors, former coworkers, or long-term professional connections. A simple question like, "Do you know any podcasts that might be a good fit for me?" can open unexpected doors, especially when you are clear about the audience you want to reach.

Most people are more willing to help than you expect. You just have to ask.

When It Is Time to Move On

If you have gone through the steps in this chapter and still cannot find contact information for a specific podcast, it may be time to redirect your efforts. Not every show is active. Some take long breaks, others do not accept guests, and a few simply never respond.

I give myself a fifteen minute time limit when searching for contact information. If I cannot find anything within that window, I shift my focus elsewhere. It is easy to fall into a time wasting rabbit hole, and that is not a good use of your outreach energy.

The reality is that many podcasts will not reply. Do not take it personally. Larger shows often receive hundreds of pitches each week and cannot respond to everyone.

The podcasts that are a good fit for you are usually easier to find, open to guests, and responsive. Once you identify those shows, the real work begins, reaching out the right way.

Why This Matters

Finding the right contact matters more than sending more pitches. Even the best message fails if it never reaches the person who can say yes.

We want to avoid wasted effort by showing you how to identify the right decision maker, use smart search tactics, and move on quickly when a show is not responsive. When your outreach reaches the right inbox, your chances of getting a reply increase immediately.

Action Step: Build a Clean Contact List

Choose five podcasts from your priority list and locate the best contact for each one. Use the methods in this chapter in order.

Start with search operators, then check the website, social media profiles, podcast directories, former guests, email lookup tools, and your personal network. Set a fifteen minute limit per podcast. Once that time is up, either log a solid contact or stop.

Create a simple tracking document and record the podcast name, contact person, contact method, and where you found it. Do not send pitches yet. The goal is accuracy, not volume.

With the right contact identified, the next step is making sure your message lands. In the next chapter, we will focus on crafting a podcast pitch that captures attention and gets replies.

Bonus Resource: Podcast Contact Research Checklist

To make this process easier, I created a contact research checklist you can use for every podcast you evaluate. It walks you through each method step by step so you do not miss obvious opportunities or waste time chasing dead ends.

Access it here:

seooptimizers.com/bonus

Or scan the QR code below for instant access.

CRAFTING A PODCAST PITCH THAT GETS REPLIES

Most podcast pitches fail not because they are bad, but because they do not clearly show value to the host.

"You can have everything in life you want, if you will just help enough other people get what they want."
— Zig Ziglar

Now that you know which podcasts are worth targeting and how to reach them, it's time to put yourself in front of the host. Your pitch is the first impression, and in most cases, it determines whether you get booked or ignored. If the value is not immediately clear, nothing else matters.

When I first started pitching podcasts, my response rate was terrible. I sent generic emails and hoped volume made up for it. It did not. Everything changed once I stopped talking about myself and started showing hosts how I help them and serve their audience.

In this chapter, I'm going to break down the exact strategies and email formats I've used to get booked on hundreds of podcasts. Use this as a framework, not a script. Make it your own, stay authentic, and you'll dramatically improve your chances of landing high-quality interviews.

The Anatomy of a Strong Pitch

There is a process behind writing a great podcast pitch. One that gets opened, gets read, and gets you booked.

A basic pitch might land you a spot on a small show. But if you want to appear on podcasts with loyal audiences and real influence, you need to stand out from the very first sentence.

I have broken this process down into ten key elements. This is the exact framework I have used to get booked on hundreds of podcasts, from niche industry shows to large platforms. The more you personalize it and make it your own, the better your results will be.

Make It Personal

Generic pitches do not get responses. If your message looks like it was copied and sent to fifty other podcasts, it is going straight to the archive. Or worse, spam.

Start with the host's name. Mention their podcast. Even better, reference something specific you genuinely liked. An episode you listened to. A guest they interviewed. A moment that stood out. This is not about flattery. It is about showing that you care, that you did your homework, and that you respect their time.

When I first started pitching podcasts, I sent the same message to everyone. It usually sounded like this: "Hey, I think your show is a great fit for me as a guest."

I thought I was saving time. What I was really doing was getting ignored. Once I started personalizing my introductions, even just one or two lines that were specific to the show, my response rate tripled.

Establish Credibility Without Overselling

Next, introduce yourself. Quickly. This is not your full bio. Just enough to make them lean in. Think of it like a podcast elevator pitch.

What makes you qualified to speak on their show? What have you done that signals you have something valuable to share with their audience?

Credibility is not about impressing the host. It is about making them feel confident saying yes. You might say something like this:

"I'm Brandon Leibowitz, founder of SEO Optimizers. Since 2007, I have helped thousands of small businesses rank higher on Google and generate more leads. I also run a digital marketing MeetUp with over 7,000 members."

That is enough. It tells them who you are, why you are credible, and that you have an audience. Hosts care about this because guests who promote their episodes help grow the show.

You do not need to name drop clients or list every stage you have spoken on. Save that for the conversation. Lead with just enough proof to show that you know what you are doing.

Show Why You're Relevant to Their Audience

When you pitch a podcast, you need to explain why you are the right fit for their audience. What can you bring to the table that their listeners actually want to hear? What topics do you know well enough to speak on with confidence?

For me, it is digital marketing. That is my lane. I am happy to talk about SEO, AI, content marketing, paid ads, social media, or anything tied to growing visibility online. I will go on broader marketing shows too, but only if there is a clear way to connect the conversation back to digital.

I do not appear on podcasts focused only on real estate unless the discussion centers on how realtors use online marketing to attract more buyers and sellers.

Stick with what you know. I have been on hundreds of marketing podcasts, and that consistency has helped me build a clear reputation. People know exactly what I do and what I stand for.

If I started jumping onto podcasts in unrelated niches, I come across as a generalist. That waters down your message. But when you stay focused on one niche, you position yourself as the go to expert. And that is how you stand out.

Share Specific Topics to Make the Host's Job Easy

When you pitch a podcast, do not just say you want to be a guest. Give the host a few specific topic ideas they can use right away. The easier you make their job, the better your chances of getting booked.

When I reach out to shows, I always include a few SEO related topics. I tailor them to the podcast's audience. If the listeners are beginners, I stick to foundational concepts. If the audience is more advanced, I go deeper. You have to match your message to who is listening.

It is about showing that you understand their audience. Hosts are always thinking in episode titles. Give them ideas they can picture on their feed.

I also keep my pitches fresh by paying attention to what is happening right now. When AI started taking off, I did not keep sending the same SEO topics I had used for years.

I started pitching ideas like:

- How AI Is Changing SEO
- Will AI Replace SEO Specialists?
- What Google Is Doing to Compete With ChatGPT

Topics like these stand out because they feel timely and relevant. They are not what everyone else is pitching, and that gets attention.

When a host scrolls through their episode list and sees something different, it makes people want to click. That leads to more listens, more shares, and more people discovering who you are and what you do.

Show Your Passion and Depth

If you are genuinely passionate about your topic, let it show. That energy can be the difference between a pitch that gets ignored and one that gets you booked. Do not just say you are interested. Show that you live and breathe the subject.

When I pitch myself to marketing podcasts, I go beyond the basics. I often mention that I started in 2007 and have years of experience. That helps, but it is not enough on its own.

What really grabs attention is when I talk about what I do outside of client work. I mention the marketing classes I teach, my podcast, my YouTube channel, my blog, and my speaking gigs. All of that signals that I am deeply involved in digital marketing, not just working in it.

Podcast hosts are looking for enthusiasm and insight. Someone who brings depth. Someone with real experience and perspectives their audience will learn from. When you show that you are a subject matter expert, not just a fan of the topic, you become a much easier yes.

Make Scheduling Easy

Let the host know you are flexible and easy to work with. Ask if they have a scheduling link or calendar where you can book a time. If they do not, offer a few dates and time slots that work for you.

The easier you make it for them, the more likely they are to say yes. Hosts are busy. Anything you can do to remove back and forth helps your pitch stand out.

Keep time zones in mind. You will be pitching podcasts all over the world. Since I am based in Los Angeles, I have adjusted my schedule many times to line up with hosts in different regions. Sometimes that means recording early in the morning or later at night.

It does not happen every time, but when it does, I make it work. Flexibility shows respect for the host's time, and that goes a long way when they are deciding who to book.

Show You've Been There, Done That

Podcast hosts get a lot of pitches. If yours does not stand out, it gets skipped. One of the easiest ways to separate yourself from everyone else is to show that you have done this before.

When I reach out, I include links to past podcast interviews, videos, or conferences I have spoken at. Anything that shows I have experience talking about digital marketing. This proves I know my stuff and makes it easier for the host to say yes.

Let's be honest. Most hosts do not want to take a chance on someone who has never been behind a microphone. Just like you probably do not want to be the first guest on a brand new show, hosts prefer guests who have already done a few interviews. It lowers the risk and gives them confidence that you will be a solid guest.

Use Podcast Clips as Social Proof

Once you understand that experience builds trust, the next step is packaging that experience the right way.

As you build a library of podcast clips, use them to land more interviews. When a host can see you speak clearly, share real value, and hold attention, it removes any doubt about whether you will be a strong guest.

Inside your pitch email, include one or two links to your best moments. Think of it like a speaker reel, but simpler and more personal. Even one strong clip is enough to build confidence.

These clips show that you are prepared, professional, and engaging. When hosts can see that proof, your outreach converts at a much higher rate.

Make It Easy to Reach You

When you pitch yourself, do not make the host guess how to get in touch. Give them your email, your phone number, or both. Whatever you are comfortable with, make it obvious.

Use a professional email address. When I first started doing outreach, I tested both my business email and a personal Gmail account. Every time I used Gmail, my response rate dropped. It simply did not feel as credible.

Now I stick with my business email, and I use one with my name on it, brandon@seooptimizers.com. Not info@. Not marketing@. It signals there is a real person behind the pitch. That small choice can be the difference between getting a reply and being ignored.

Watch Your Grammar It Matters

Before you hit send on a podcast pitch, take a minute to clean it up. Spelling mistakes, awkward grammar, and sloppy sentences make you look unprepared. If you are asking to be featured on someone's show, that is not the impression you want to leave. There are plenty of tools that can help, but even reading your email out loud will catch most mistakes.

Think about it from the host's perspective. A pitch that is clear and polished signals effort and professionalism. Do not let something as simple as a typo or poor punctuation be the reason you do not get a response. Clean it up, keep it sharp, and always send your best.

Don't Be Afraid to Follow Up

If you do not hear back right away, do not take it personally. Many podcasts receive hundreds of pitches, and your message may get buried or opened later. A thoughtful follow up can make a real difference.

Timing matters. Following up a few weeks, or even a couple of months later, keeps your message from feeling pushy while still putting you back on the host's radar. Reaching out again after just a few days can hurt your chances more than it helps.

When you follow up, keep it brief and respectful. You do not need to restate your entire pitch. Ask if they have any upcoming openings that might be a fit and let them know you are open to being considered in the future.

If the answer is no, thank them for their time and leave the door open. Let them know you would be happy to reconnect if the timing or direction of the show changes. That professionalism is remembered.

This is a quality over quantity game. You are better off landing a few great podcast appearances than blasting out dozens of pitches. Be patient, stay professional, and keep your outreach focused. A well handled follow up shows confidence, respect, and persistence, which are exactly the qualities podcast hosts look for in guests.

Email Templates That Work

Below, I've included a few pitch templates to help you get started. These are based on what I've used myself.

Do not copy and paste them word for word. Use them as a starting point. Adjust the language, add your personality, and make sure each message sounds like you. That is what turns a decent pitch into one that actually gets booked.

Sample Template 1: General Outreach Email

Subject: Guest Inquiry for [Podcast Name]
Hi [Podcast Host/Producer's Name],
I'm [Your Name], and I wanted to reach out about being a guest on your show, [Podcast Name].

I have been following the podcast and really enjoyed [mention a specific episode, guest, or something unique about their show]. My background in [briefly share your niche or expertise] aligns well with your audience and adds real value for listeners.
I've attached my bio and a few topic ideas I speak on. I'm also happy to answer any questions or provide more info if needed. You can check out some of my past podcast appearances here: [link to podcasts].
If this sounds like a good fit, I'd love to work out a time to record. I'll make sure to share the episode with my audience as well.
Thanks for considering it,
[Your Full Name]
[Your Contact Info]

Sample Template 2: Topic Specific Pitch

Subject: Interview Topic Idea for [Podcast Name] on [Your Niche]
Hi [Podcast Host/Producer's Name],
Hope you're doing well. I wanted to reach out with an interview idea that is a great fit for your audience at [Podcast Name].
My name is [Your Name], and I've been working in [your field or niche] for [X years]. I focus on [brief focus area or niche expertise], and I've spoken on podcasts and at events about [relevant topics].
One thing I like about your show is how you make complex ideas simple. Like in your episode with [mention specific guest or episode]. That's the kind of platform I'd love to contribute to.
I've attached a few talking points that resonate with your listeners. I've also linked to some past interviews so you can get a sense of my speaking style.
If it seems like a fit, I'd love to work out a time to chat. And of course, I'll promote the episode to my audience so we both get some extra reach.
Thanks again,

[Your Full Name]
[Your Contact Info]
[Your Website or LinkedIn]

Sample Template 3: Story Driven Pitch

Subject: A Story I'd Love to Share with Your Audience
Hi [Podcast Host/Producer's Name],
Thanks for taking a second to read this. I'm [Your Name], and I wanted to reach out with a personal story I think really clicks with your audience at [Podcast Name].
A while back, I [share quick summary of the story or key event]. It wasn't easy, but it taught me a ton about [what you learned or how it connects to your field]. Since then, I've used that experience to [what you now do as a result], and I think your audience will take a lot from it too.
I've been featured on other podcasts and stages talking about [mention similar topics], and I've found that storytelling is one of the best ways to connect with listeners. I'm attaching my bio and a few ideas for what we can cover during the episode.
Also including links to past interviews so you can hear my approach. I'd be excited to share this message with your audience and help promote the episode to mine as well.
Appreciate your time,
[Your Full Name]
[Your Contact Info]
[Website or socials]

Editing Your Pitch Before Sending

Before you hit send, take the time to edit your pitch. This is where clarity, conciseness, and professionalism matter most. You need to grab attention quickly, communicate value clearly, and end with a strong call to action (CTA). This is your moment to stand out and earn the booking.

The templates above are a starting point, not a finished product. Do not send them as is. Edit them to match your voice and your experience. Add details that are specific to you and relevant to the show you are pitching.

The more you personalize and refine your pitch, the higher your chances of getting booked. Small edits make a big difference, especially when hosts are scanning emails and deciding who gets a reply.

Edit for Clarity, Conciseness, and Professionalism

Treat your pitch like a professional email. Remove anything that does not add value. Keep it short and focused so you do not lose the reader's attention. Always take the time to proofread before sending.

Even a few extra minutes of editing can make or break a pitch. Spelling mistakes or grammatical errors signal a lack of care and can instantly hurt your credibility. If proofreading is not your strength, use a tool or friend to catch anything you might miss.

Clean, polished pitches stand out. Sloppy ones get skipped.

Catch Their Attention

When you write a podcast pitch, remember that you are competing with a sea of other emails from people who all want the same thing. To be featured on the show.

Put real effort into your pitch. The more personalized, interesting, and specific it feels, the better your chances of getting a response.

Always tailor your pitch to the podcast and the host. Think about their audience, interests, and tone. If you know the host's name, use it. Including their name in the subject line or opening sentence makes the email feel relevant and worth opening.

This may require a little detective work, but it is worth it. Spend time on the podcast's website and social media channels. Look at past episodes, guest topics, and how the host communicates. I covered how to do this in the previous chapter.

I receive podcast pitches all the time. Most of them look the same and are easy to skim past. The ones I actually read usually have one thing in common. They start by addressing me by name and referencing something specific about my work. That immediately catches my attention.

I use the same approach in my own outreach. The more personal the message, the better the response rate.

Call to Action

Like any strong pitch, your email needs to end with a clear CTA. Make it obvious what you want the host to do next and make it easy for them to do it. Encourage them to reply, schedule a call, or book a recording time. Include clear contact information and be ready to respond when they reach out.

Your goal is to remove confusion. Make it immediately clear why you are emailing, what you are asking for, and how the host can move forward if they are interested in having you on the show.

Not every pitch will get a yes. Some will get a no. Others will not get a response at all. That is part of the process. When this happens, stay professional and do not take it personally. Handle rejections politely, learn from them when possible, and keep moving forward.

Consistent, respectful follow up and clear calls to action are what turn outreach into bookings over time.

Be Professional and Express Gratitude

If you are rejected, handle it professionally. Respond politely, thank them for their time, and keep the door open for future opportunities. Let them know you are available down the road, and if it feels appropriate, ask them to keep you in mind or pass your contact information along to others who may be a better fit.

Express genuine gratitude. Stay respectful and positive. Consider subscribing to their podcast or connecting on social media as a simple show of good faith. Offering support or assistance within your expertise is another way to build trust and leave a strong impression.

How you handle rejection matters more than most people realize. Podcast hosts talk to each other. A rude or dismissive response can spread just as easily as a good one. This applies beyond podcasting as well. Treat people the way you want to be treated.

A podcast that says no today may say yes later. I once had a host reach out two years after rejecting my initial pitch. At the time, they were overloaded with digital marketing guests and wanted to change direction. Years later, they decided to bring digital marketing back into the mix. Because I handled the rejection professionally, I was one of the first people they contacted.

Leaving things on a positive note increases the chances that the right opportunity finds its way back to you.

Don't Give Up

Rejection is a natural part of the process. When handled the right way, it can still lead to future opportunities. Do not take a no personally or let it discourage you. Rejections and successes go hand in hand when you put yourself out there. What matters most is how you respond to them.

Treat each rejection as a learning opportunity. If you are not getting much traction, consider asking for feedback. Some hosts will not respond, but others may share insight that helps you improve future pitches.

As you gain experience sending pitches and receiving replies, you will get more comfortable knowing what works. Strong pitches are personalized, clearly explain your expertise, show relevance to the podcast, and demonstrate familiarity with the show. That combination is what gets attention.

You also need to clearly communicate what you bring to the table that others do not. Make it clear why you are the right choice. Learning how to sell your experience and value quickly is an essential skill.

Your hook matters. Hosts scan emails fast. Keep your pitches short, focused, and free of unnecessary tangents. Clear, concise messages perform better than long explanations.

You may have noticed that the templates include a brief line offering to promote the episode. This is intentional. Some podcasts charge a fee for guest appearances. Offering to share the episode with your audience can sometimes be enough incentive to waive or reduce that fee.

I have personally shown hosts my social media profiles and email subscriber numbers and had four figure podcasting fees waived. This does not work every time, but it is a strong negotiating tool. If you can bring exposure, hosts are often more flexible.

Even when fees are not waived, offering promotion increases your chances of getting a positive response. Building an audience you can share episodes with is one of the most valuable assets you can have as a podcast guest.

Many people underestimate the power of a strong email list. If you build a list through a lead magnet and consistently share podcast appearances with your subscribers, hosts are more likely to invite you back or recommend you to other shows.

Why This Matters

Podcast hosts are not looking for more pitches. They are looking for the right guest. Every element you learned in this chapter is designed to remove friction and build confidence on the host's side.

Personalization shows respect. Clear positioning shows relevance. Specific topics show preparation. Proof of experience reduces risk. Professional follow up builds trust.

When you put all of this together, your pitch stops feeling like an interruption and starts feeling like an opportunity. That is how you move from getting ignored to getting booked on podcasts that actually matter.

Action Step: Send One High-Quality Pitch

Do not try to pitch ten podcasts today. Choose one. Pick a podcast from your short list and write a pitch using the framework from this chapter.

Before you send it, make sure it includes:

- A personalized opening that references the host or show
- A clear explanation of why you are relevant to their audience
- Two or three specific topic ideas
- Proof of experience or clips if available
- A clear CTA that makes it easy to reply or schedule

Send one thoughtful, well crafted pitch today. Quality beats volume every time.

Now that you know how to identify the right podcasts, find the right contact, and craft pitches that get replies, it's time to focus on the interview itself. In the next chapter, I'll show you how to show up as a confident, prepared guest and deliver an interview that actually moves the needle.

Bonus Resource: Podcast Outreach Checklist

To help you book podcasts more consistently, I created a podcast outreach checklist you can use for every pitch. These are the same frameworks I use in my own outreach.

Access it here:

seooptimizers.com/bonus

Or scan the QR code below for instant access.

PART 2

THE PERFORMANCE
(DELIVERING LIKE A PRO)

DIALING IN YOUR TECH AND LOGISTICS LIKE A PRO

Create a fail-proof environment so you can walk into every interview calm, prepared, and professional.

"By failing to prepare, you are preparing to fail."
— Benjamin Franklin

By now, you've got the tools to start booking yourself on podcasts. You know how to find the right shows, pitch your story, and land interviews. But that's only half the process. Now it's time to show up ready.

In this chapter, I'll walk you through exactly what to do before you ever hit record. You'll learn how to lock in the details, prepare your space, and dial in your tech so you can walk into every interview calm, focused, and professional.

Preparation is not optional. It is what separates a forgettable interview from a professional one.

To show up ready, you need to:

- Confirm all logistics in advance
- Set up a clean, professional recording space
- Run a full technical check before the interview

Let's get you set up so nothing catches you off guard when it's time to record.

Confirming Logistics

Once you get a yes from a podcast host, do not wait around. Respond quickly and professionally to lock in the interview and confirm the details. How you handle this back and forth sets the tone for how you will show up as a guest.

Before every interview, there are three things I always make sure to confirm:

1. Clear communication with the host
2. The show's format and expectations
3. The date, time, and time zone, sometimes with a short pre interview chat

If a host skips these steps or seems disorganized, take note. They may be new to podcasting or simply not running a polished operation. That is not always a dealbreaker, but remember that the goal is quality over quantity.

You want to appear on podcasts that reflect well on you, sound professional, and attract the right audience.

Communicate With the Host

I have had hosts send me their booking link only to find that the next available slot was six months out. I booked it anyway, but a few weeks before the interview, the host let me know they were pausing new recordings for the rest of the year. If I had responded sooner, I might have secured an earlier slot.

It is also important to remember that even after you record the interview, it may not air right away. Editing and publishing can take weeks or longer. In some cases, your episode might not go live until months later, sometimes not until the following year.

I have recorded interviews at all kinds of hours, including late at night, to accommodate hosts in different time zones. One recent interview was with a marketing podcast based in Australia. I am in Los Angeles, which means a nineteen hour time difference.

It was not ideal, but sometimes flexibility is part of reaching the right audience.

The day before every interview, I send a short confirmation email to make sure everything is still on track. Hosts are busy, schedules change, and reminders help avoid unnecessary confusion.

There have been times when I logged in, waited several minutes, and heard nothing. In those situations, I send a quick check in email and keep the recording link open while I continue working.

On more than one occasion, the host joined late after a previous meeting ran long. A simple confirmation the day before prevents that uncertainty.

Understanding the Format

Once you have locked in the basic logistics of the interview, do not stop there. You also need to understand the format so you know exactly what to expect when it is time to record.

Before every interview, I ask the host a short set of questions:

- Is the interview live or pre recorded
- Will it be one on one or part of a panel
- How long will the interview run
- Will the recording be edited or mostly raw
- Is there a live audience component
- Is the format structured with set questions or more conversational
- When will the episode go live

Skipping these questions can leave you scrambling. I have shown up expecting a relaxed conversation, only to realize I was live on a streamed panel. That early experience taught me to always clarify the format in advance.

Now, I make it a point to cover these questions in every pre interview or email thread with the host. It takes just a few minutes and removes unnecessary stress. When you know what kind of interview you are walking into, you show up focused, confident, and ready to deliver.

Once that is squared away, it is time to set up your space and dial in your tech.

Pre Interview Discussions and Final Confirmation

If possible, schedule a short pre interview with the host. This is a great way to align on the main themes of the episode, clarify any specific topics they want to cover, and flag ideas or stories you like to include.

Most hosts will ask if there is anything you want to make sure gets mentioned. Use that moment intentionally. This is not about scripting the conversation. It is about making sure the interview is aligned and valuable for their audience.

For example, with AI being such a hot topic in marketing right now, I will often suggest including a few questions about how AI is changing digital strategy. Timely topics like this tend to spark better conversations and increase listener engagement.

Before the interview, send the host a short bio, a professional headshot, and links to your website and social channels. Keep your bio concise. Two to five sentences is more than enough. Most hosts will not read anything longer. I keep everything in a simple one page document so I can send it quickly and make the host's job easier.

Once the date and time are confirmed, block the interview on your calendar and build in extra buffer time. I leave at least thirty minutes open before and after the scheduled recording. If the interview starts late or runs long, I am not rushing or distracted.

I have been on shows where the host was running behind. When there is communication, it is not a problem. Having buffer time gives the conversation room to flow without stress.

The goal of this step is alignment and readiness. When expectations are clear and logistics are finalized, you can focus fully on showing up and delivering value.

Next, let's look at how to set up a professional, distraction free space so you are ready the moment the recording starts.

Prepare Your Space and Gear

Do not overlook this step. Your podcast setup does not need to be fancy, but it does need to sound and look professional. At a minimum, use something better than your computer's built-in microphone and webcam.

Your environment matters just as much as your equipment. Choose a quiet space where you will not be interrupted. Avoid barking dogs, doorbells, or background noise. A clean, distraction free setup helps you come across as polished and prepared, both in sound and appearance.

Assessing Interview Location

If your interview will be recorded at a studio or at someone else's location, do not hesitate to ask about logistics and equipment ahead of time. Familiarize yourself with the gear they will be using, and speak up if anything is unclear, especially if you will be working with equipment you have not used before.

That said, most podcast interviews today are recorded virtually from home. If you are setting up your own space, the next steps will help you create a podcast ready environment that sounds great and feels professional.

Microphone, Webcam, and Lighting

If you are doing interviews from home, it is worth investing in a solid setup. You do not need a full studio, but you do need to sound clear and look professional. A few smart upgrades can make a noticeable difference in how you show up on camera and on the mic.

There are three pieces of gear I recommend for every podcast guest:

- A high quality microphone
- A high definition webcam
- Reliable lighting

Do not skip any of these. They may seem like small details, but they play a major role in how hosts and listeners perceive you. Clear audio and clean visuals signal professionalism and make it easier for your message to land.

My Early Setup

When I first started guesting on podcasts, I was using my laptop's built in webcam, a budget external microphone, and no lighting at all. It technically worked, but just barely.

After listening back to a few episodes, I cringed. The audio had an echo. I sounded distant. The video was dark and pixelated. I did not look or sound like someone who was taking this seriously, and that matters.

The first upgrade I made was a proper webcam and microphone. The improvement was immediate. I looked sharper and sounded clearer. But something still felt off. I had not thought much about lighting.

After recording a few more interviews, I noticed how flat and shadowy the video looked. That is when it clicked. Lighting was the missing piece.

I picked up two softbox lights, and the difference was dramatic. I finally looked like I belonged on camera. It did not cost a fortune, but it was intentional, and that made all the difference.

What Makes a Difference

The right microphone brings out the clarity and fullness of your voice. A USB microphone is easy to use and plugs directly into your computer with no complicated setup. The goal is to reduce echo, limit background noise, and avoid the hollow sound that built in microphones often produce.

Built in laptop cameras are usually low resolution and poorly lit. A high definition webcam sharpens your image, improves motion clarity, and helps you come across more clearly on screen. You will also use it for Zoom calls, content videos, and webinars, so it is not just a podcast investment.

Lighting is the most overlooked upgrade. Natural light can work, but it is inconsistent. Proper lighting gives you control over brightness, warmth, and direction, which makes your space look intentional rather than accidental.

The result is simple. You show up polished, credible, and confident, and that confidence translates into trust with both the host and the audience.

Do I Really Need All This

I get it. When you are just starting out, investing in gear might not feel urgent. But the reality is that podcasting is part of your brand. These interviews live online long after they are recorded. Every time someone hears your voice or sees your face, they are forming an impression. Why not make it a strong one?

Good gear does not have to be expensive. You can build a reliable setup for a few hundred dollars or less. Once it is in place, you do not have to think about it again. Your setup works for you in the background while you focus on delivering value.

Create a Distraction-Free Space

Once your gear is set, the next step is preparing your physical space. You want an environment that is clear, quiet, and free from distractions. One that allows you to show up focused and confident.

You are creating the conditions for a strong conversation. Give yourself the space to focus, stay present, and bring your best energy to the interview.

Soundproofing Tips on a Budget

If outside noise is an issue, consider a few simple soundproofing upgrades. Heavy curtains, rugs, acoustic panels, or even bookshelves filled with soft materials can noticeably improve how your room sounds.

When I first started guest podcasting, I recorded in a room near a busy street. I dealt with everything from sirens to leaf blowers to birds chirping during interviews. It was not ideal. I quickly realized that if I wanted to sound professional, I needed a quieter space.

Most podcast microphones do a good job of isolating your voice, but do not rely on the mic alone. Reduce background noise as much as possible so nothing interferes with the conversation.

Set the Right Visual Tone

Your background matters. A simple, intentional setup goes a long way. You can showcase a book you have written, your logo, or other subtle brand elements. Keep it clean and minimal. Too much clutter looks chaotic and draws attention away from your message.

If you do not have a strong visual background, you can blur it or use a virtual background. Just make sure it looks clean and stable and does not glitch or compete for attention.

Your background does not need to be flashy. It needs to be thoughtful. Whether it is real or virtual, it reinforces credibility and keeps the focus on you.

Minimize Digital Distractions

Before your interview, silence or turn off anything that could interrupt you. Even a single notification can break your focus and disrupt the flow of the conversation.

Make sure to shut down:

- Phones
- Email programs
- Slack or other messaging platforms
- Social media tabs
- Any software that triggers pop-ups or alerts

I learned this the hard way early on. I was working on a Facebook Ads campaign for a client right before an interview and forgot to close the tab. A few minutes in, I heard a notification. Then another. It was not until the third alert that I realized the sound was coming from my own computer.

I had to stop the interview, ask the host to pause, and close Facebook. Thankfully, it was not a live recording, so the moment was edited out. In a live setting, that interruption becomes a problem.

Now, I only keep two things open during an interview: the recording platform and my notes. Nothing else.

A quiet digital setup is not just polite. It is professional. It shows respect for the host's time and allows you to stay present and deliver value.

Technical Check and Troubleshooting

Technical issues can throw off your confidence, frustrate the host, and waste valuable time. I have dealt with nearly every glitch imaginable, from internet outages to webcams failing to connect, to a laptop shutting down mid interview.

That is why I always run through a short checklist ahead of time. In the sections that follow, I will walk you through what to test and how to avoid common mistakes I learned the hard way.

Technical Checks

Before every interview, take time to double check your equipment. Even small issues can disrupt the recording, waste everyone's time, or force an unnecessary reschedule.

Start with your microphone. Make sure it is working properly and capturing your voice clearly. Record a short test clip and listen back for clarity, volume, and background noise. Position the microphone correctly based on its pickup pattern. If you are using a cardioid microphone, speak into the front, not the top or side.

Next, test your webcam and lighting. Look for common issues such as:

- Focus problems
- Overexposure or underexposure
- Uneven lighting or harsh shadows
- Incorrect color balance
- Framing that is too close, too far, or off center

Even lighting across your face helps you appear clear and professional on camera. You can quickly test both your audio and video by opening a meeting in Zoom or Google Meet, recording a short clip, and playing it back.

Finally, confirm which recording platform the host will be using. Some hosts rely on Zoom, while others prefer platforms such as Riverside for higher quality audio and video. If you are not familiar with the platform, take time to test it in advance so you feel confident when it is time to record.

What Experience Taught Me

I recently bought a new 4K webcam and expected it to work as soon as I plugged it in. I was booked on a live show, and when it was time to start, the webcam did not connect. It showed it was on, but no video came through.

We had to stop the interview and reschedule. It was frustrating for both of us and completely avoidable.

A quick test beforehand saves time and stress. Learn from my mistake and do not assume new gear works perfectly without testing it first.

Pre Interview Troubleshooting

Sometimes things do not go as planned, even when you have done everything right. That is why it is important to know how to troubleshoot common issues before you go live.

If something is not working during your tech check, try these quick fixes:

- Restart your modem or router to stabilize your internet connection
- Close unnecessary apps or browser tabs to free up bandwidth and system memory
- Restart your computer or device
- Check all cable connections, as loose plugs are a common issue
- Update your audio and video drivers and confirm your operating system is current
- Update the recording software or browser you will be using
- Have a backup plan, such as a second device ready in case something fails

Running these checks ahead of time can turn potential problems into minor inconveniences. It only takes a few minutes, but it can save you from missed interviews, unnecessary stress, or damage to your professional reputation. A small amount of preparation now can save hours of frustration later.

Why This Matters

Podcast hosts notice preparation immediately. When you show up on time, understand the format, sound clear, and look professional, you build trust before you ever say a word. That trust leads to better conversations, stronger relationships with hosts, and more impactful interviews that live online long after the recording ends.

Preparation also removes stress. When your space, gear, and tech are dialed in, you can focus on the conversation instead of worrying about what might go wrong. The more prepared you are before hitting record, the more confident and natural you will sound once the interview begins.

Action Step: Create a Pre Interview Checklist

Before your next podcast interview, create a simple pre interview checklist that includes:

- Confirming the date, time, and time zone
- Reviewing the interview format
- Testing your microphone, camera, and lighting
- Preparing a quiet, distraction free space
- Blocking buffer time on your calendar

Use this checklist before every interview so preparation becomes automatic instead of rushed.

When your logistics are confirmed, your space is dialed in, and your tech works without thinking about it, you give yourself a real advantage. Preparation lets you focus on what actually matters: the conversation.

In the next chapter, we'll move beyond setup and into execution. You'll learn how to show up on the mic, deliver real value, and turn every interview into a memorable experience for the host and the audience.

Bonus Resource: Podcast Guest Gear and Setup Guide

To help you get set up quickly, I put together a curated guide with microphones, webcams, lighting setups, and basic tech recommendations I trust, with options for different budgets. This resource is updated regularly so you can make smart choices without spending hours researching.

Access it here:

seooptimizers.com/bonus

Or scan the QR code below for instant access.

RESEARCH AND MESSAGING THAT WOWS THE HOST

Analyze the show, shape your story, and deliver value in a way listeners remember.

"Confidence comes from being prepared."
— John Wooden

Testing your equipment and setting up your recording space are important, but preparing your mindset matters just as much. You do not want to jump into a podcast feeling rushed, scattered, or uncertain. You want to show up focused, confident, and clear on your story.

Take a few minutes before the interview to reset. Step outside for fresh air. Do a short stretch or take a quick walk. I like to meditate for a few minutes before I record. It helps me shift out of work mode, clear mental clutter, and bring my full attention to the conversation.

That brief reset helps me tune in to what I want to share and often sparks new ideas or angles I had not considered.

Podcasting is not just about answering questions. It is about connection, presence, and sharing something meaningful. When you show up mentally sharp, you speak with more clarity, confidence, and ease.

And part of being mentally prepared is knowing what you are walking into. That starts with doing a little homework on the podcast itself.

Researching the Show

Once your space is set up and your tech is ready, it is time to do your homework. Before stepping into any interview, make sure you understand the podcast you are joining. This preparation helps you avoid surprises and show up with confidence.

Early on, I skipped this step for a show I assumed would be straightforward. I jumped in thinking it was a casual marketing conversation, only to realize halfway through that the audience was made up of advanced agency owners.

My examples felt too basic, and I had to adjust on the fly. That interview taught me a clear lesson. A few minutes of research upfront prevents scrambling mid conversation and boosts your confidence.

Start with the basics:

- Who is the host
- Who is the target audience
- What type of guests does the show typically feature
- What is the overall tone of the conversation

Spend time with a few past episodes. Notice how the host asks questions, how long the conversations usually run, and whether the show follows a consistent structure.

Some podcasts end each episode with a standard set of questions, like advice for their younger self or a book that changed their life. Knowing these patterns ahead of time helps you prepare thoughtful responses that resonate with listeners.

There are also common questions that appear on nearly every show, including how you got started, your biggest challenge, or your most meaningful success. Later in this chapter, we will cover how to prepare strong stories and talking points so you are never caught off guard.

Understand the Host

Taking time to understand the host's background, interests, and expertise can make your interview smoother and more engaging. The more you know in advance, the more natural the conversation will feel.

During your preparation, you may uncover personal details or shared interests. Referencing those during the interview shows the host that you came prepared and creates an immediate connection.

I am an avid skateboarder, and while researching a podcast I was booked on, I noticed the host had several skateboarding photos on Instagram. I brought it up during the interview, and we ended up spending time talking about skateboarding. That naturally led into a conversation about how I built a skateboard company called Shralpin using social media and marketing.

That type of connection makes the interview more memorable and helps you stand out as a guest.

To get a better feel for the host, spend about fifteen minutes doing the following:

- Review their social media profiles
- Listen to podcasts where they have appeared as a guest
- Read blogs, newsletters, or articles they have written
- Visit websites they manage or are affiliated with

Search their name and company across platforms such as LinkedIn, YouTube, Instagram, X, and TikTok.

You do not need to memorize their full background. Having a general sense of their voice, values, and content style is enough.

This extra preparation helps the conversation flow, builds rapport quickly, and increases the chances that the host will want to invite you back.

Research the Audience

Before any podcast interview, take a moment to ask who is actually listening to the show. Understanding the audience is essential if you want your message to land.

Look into the podcast's listener demographics, including age, industry, goals, and experience level. Tailor your content to match what they care about while still staying true to your voice.

When you take the time to understand who you are speaking to, you naturally adjust how you frame your story, which examples you choose, and the tone you use.

For example, when I am booked on a show for first time entrepreneurs, I focus on relatable struggles and practical advice from building my business. When the audience is made up of experienced executives, I shift toward strategy and data driven insights.

The core message stays the same. The delivery changes.

I once went into an interview planning to share high level growth strategies, only to realize within the first few minutes that the audience was mostly people just getting started. Instead of pushing forward, I slowed down and simplified my examples, focusing on early wins and common mistakes.

The energy shifted almost immediately, and the feedback afterward was overwhelmingly positive. That experience reinforced that adaptability often matters more than sticking rigidly to a plan.

When I know the audience in advance, preparation makes an even bigger difference. I appeared on a podcast for authors and shaped my examples around selling books online. I walked through platforms like Amazon, website optimization, and third party distribution channels. That approach connected far better than keeping the conversation generic.

How to Research the Listener Base

Start by reviewing the podcast's description. Most hosts clearly explain who the show is for, such as coaches, solopreneurs, real estate agents, or startup founders.

Next, scan recent episode titles and descriptions. Look for patterns in guest types, recurring topics, and themes that appear often.

Finally, check audience engagement. Notice which episodes receive more views, reviews, or shares. These signals offer clues about what resonates most with listeners.

As you prepare, ask yourself:

- What will this audience find inspiring, useful, or unexpected?
- Are there any terms or concepts that need simplification or explanation?
- Which stories or examples will feel most relatable to them?

The better you understand who you are speaking to, the easier it becomes to shape a message that connects, sticks, and gets shared.

Listen to Previous Episodes

One of the best ways to prepare for a podcast interview is by listening to a few past episodes. This gives you a clear sense of how the show flows and how the host interacts with guests.

Pay close attention to:

- The interviewing style, whether it is structured, conversational, or spontaneous
- How guests introduce themselves
- The tone and pacing of the conversation
- The typical episode length and overall structure

Many hosts will ask if you have listened to the show before. When you can reference something specific from a previous episode, such as a topic, a guest, or even a moment that stood out, it shows the host that you did your homework. That small effort can quickly build trust and rapport.

If you do not have time to listen to a full episode, review a few segments or scan recent episode titles and descriptions. Even that level of preparation can reveal valuable clues about the audience, format, and expectations.

Look for recurring themes, guest types, or values the show consistently promotes. The more familiar you are with the podcast's style, the easier it becomes to tailor your delivery and connect with listeners.

This simple step often makes the difference between a good interview and a great one.

Building Your Talking Points and Stories

Now that you have confirmed the logistics and developed a strong grasp of the podcast's tone, audience, and format, it is time to focus on what you will share during the interview. This is where preparation turns into real impact.

A guest podcast appearance is not just about answering questions. It is about telling a story that connects with listeners. Your story needs to be informative, engaging, and relatable. When done well, it can turn listeners into long-term followers and, in many cases, future customers.

The goal is to shape your message with intention. Define a few core talking points that support your goals. Use real world examples to bring your experience to life. Highlight what makes your perspective different so the audience understands why your story matters.

You also want to build credibility without sounding scripted. That means speaking with clarity and confidence while staying flexible enough to adapt to the host's style and the flow of the conversation.

Whether you are sharing a personal journey, a lesson learned, or expert insights, strong preparation helps you communicate with purpose and leave a lasting impression. Your story is one of your most powerful tools. Use it intentionally.

Crafting Engaging Points

Before you record, take time to think about what you want to say and how to say it in a way that feels relatable and memorable.

Start by understanding the tone and values of the podcast. What kind of conversations does the host usually lead? What themes matter most to the audience? When your message matches the style of the show, listeners connect faster and the interview feels more natural.

To stay focused, break your message into a few core themes. These reflect your expertise and speak directly to what the audience cares about. Keep your main ideas clear, concise, and easy to remember.

When I guest on podcasts, I try to bring up topics that are timely and aligned with my strengths. Sometimes the host asks in advance if there are specific points I want to cover. That is when I suggest topics that matter right now, such as how AI is changing digital marketing and what that means for SEO.

One of the best ways to make your message land is through storytelling. Do not just share facts. Bring them to life with examples. A strong story makes your message more human, more visual, and more memorable.

What Makes a Story Stick?

Before you ever step into an interview, it helps to understand what separates stories that fade from stories that stick. The most memorable podcast moments are not perfectly polished responses. They are clear, human stories that listeners can follow, relate to, and remember.

When you understand how strong stories are structured, you can share your experiences in a way that feels natural while still delivering impact.

Strong stories follow a simple structure:

- **Beginning**: Set the scene or provide context
- **Middle**: Introduce tension, a challenge, or a turning point
- **End**: Share the outcome, insight, or result

Engage the listener's senses whenever possible. Paint a picture with your words and connect to real emotions. The more vivid and human the story, the more likely it is to resonate.

It also helps to prepare a few stories tied to questions most podcast hosts ask, such as:

- Where you are from
- How you got started
- A challenge you overcame
- One lesson that changed everything

Instead of preparing short answers, prepare full stories. A simple question like where you are from can become a personal journey that explains how you arrived at what you do today and why it matters.

You do not need a script. Preparing a few strong stories in advance allows you to speak naturally while still delivering a message that leaves a lasting impression.

Demonstrating Your Value

Now it is time to think about how you will position yourself as a credible expert and deliver real value to listeners.

Ask yourself one simple question: What do I bring to the table that no one else can?

Listeners want more than information. They want to feel that they can trust you. They are listening for authenticity, authority, and insight. With the right preparation, you can deliver all three.

Start by identifying the parts of your story that are most relevant to the audience. Which personal or professional experiences demonstrate credibility? Which examples clearly show that you know what you are talking about?

Your goal is to educate, entertain, and inspire. Share your expertise without turning the interview into a sales pitch. When you provide genuine value, listeners naturally want to learn more and take the next step on their own.

After one interview where I walked through a practical SEO framework step by step, a listener reached out saying they replayed that section twice and shared it with their team. The host later told me it became one of their most referenced episodes. I never pitched anything. I focused on being useful. That experience reinforced that value builds trust faster than promotion ever will.

Avoid promoting yourself too early. The moment an interview feels overly sales driven, trust drops. Focus instead on sharing useful insights and actionable advice. When the host opens the door by asking how people can connect with you or work with you, that is your signal to promote. We will cover how to handle that moment later in the book.

When I guest on podcasts, I often walk through step by step strategies for improving SEO and increasing search visibility. I do not hold back. I can explain technical elements such as Schema markup and backend structure, but if I go too deep, I risk losing part of the audience.

That is why I pay close attention to the experience level of the audience. With advanced listeners, I dive deeper. With newer audiences, I focus on big picture strategy.

The key is understanding the level of your audience and adjusting your delivery without watering down the message. You do not want to overwhelm beginners or bore experienced listeners. Your value comes from knowing how to meet people where they are.

Rehearsing Your Delivery

Before the interview itself, it helps to practice a few times. A mock interview with a friend, coworker, or mentor can help you get comfortable with the format and delivery. Ask for honest, constructive feedback and use it to improve your pacing, tone, and clarity.

If no one is available, practice on your own. I used to record myself to see how I looked and sounded. It was not always easy to watch, but it gave me clear insight into what worked and what did not. You can also share short practice clips on online forums for feedback, but take those opinions with perspective. Not all feedback is useful.

While practicing, focus on staying calm and speaking at a relaxed, steady pace. Avoid rushing, but also avoid speaking so slowly that you lose momentum. The goal is to sound natural and approachable.

If nerves start to show up, bring your focus back to your key messages. Keep a few notes nearby or pause for a few deep breaths to reset. Posture matters more than most people realize. I prefer standing during interviews because it feels more natural and keeps my energy up. A sit stand desk made a noticeable difference for me and has become part of my setup.

Interviews can sometimes hit a lull. When that happens, do not panic. Ask an open ended question to re-engage the host and move the conversation forward. I have done this many times when the energy dips or there is a long pause.

During one interview, while talking about Google Analytics, the conversation stalled. I asked the host if they had experienced challenges using Google Analytics. That single question opened a longer discussion about tracking frustrations and best practices and led into a useful conversation about uncovering the real value of website traffic.

Avoid yes or no questions whenever possible. They often stop momentum. Open ended questions invite deeper discussion and create new paths for the conversation.

In one of my first interviews, the host asked if I enjoyed SEO. I was nervous and responded with a quick yes. Then there was silence. Watching that interview later made me cringe. That moment taught me what not to do.

Now I answer that question by explaining why I enjoy SEO, what challenges keep me engaged, and how client success motivates my work. That type of response adds depth, keeps the conversation moving, and gives the audience something meaningful to connect with.

Practice gives you the confidence to handle those moments and turn short answers into real conversations. You are booked, prepared, and ready to deliver. Now it is time to step into the interview and deliver, without sounding forced, scripted, or sales driven.

Why This Matters

Most guests think the work is done once they get booked. It is not. The interview itself is where everything either clicks or falls flat.

This is the moment where preparation turns into authority. When you show up focused, clear, and present, you don't just answer questions. You shape the conversation, earn trust with the audience, and position yourself as the expert the host wants to highlight.

A strong interview does more than sound good. It creates memorable moments, quotable sound bites, and long-term visibility that keeps working for you long after the episode is published.

Action Step: Define Your Core Messages

Before your next interview, write down your three core messages. These are the ideas you want the listener to remember even if they only hear part of the episode.

For each message, add:

- One short story or example
- One practical takeaway the audience can apply immediately

Keep these notes nearby during the interview. You are not scripting. You are anchoring yourself so you can stay on track, stay calm, and bring consistent value no matter where the conversation goes.

Preparation sets the foundation, but how you show up in the moment is what separates a good interview from a great one. In the next chapter, we will break down how to crush the interview itself.

You will learn how to share your expertise naturally, guide the conversation with confidence, and create opportunities without turning the episode into a commercial.

Bonus Resource: Podcast Interview Prep Sheet

This is a simple one page worksheet I use before every interview. It helps you clarify your core messages, outline key stories, and prepare talking points without sounding rehearsed. You can use it ten minutes before an interview and still feel confident and in control when the mic goes live.

Access it here:

seooptimizers.com/bonus

Or scan the QR code below for instant access.

CRUSHING THE INTERVIEW WITHOUT SOUNDING SALESY

Show up confident, share stories that stick, and guide listeners to a clear next step without turning the interview into a pitch.

"Great communication begins with connection."
— Oprah Winfrey

You've done the hard work: researched shows, sent pitches, and landed interviews. Now comes the part that matters most. Showing up and delivering.

This chapter is about what happens when the mic goes live. It breaks down how to give an interview that feels natural, memorable, and genuinely valuable. You will learn how to share your expertise without turning the conversation into a pitch, connect with the host and audience, and tell your story in a way listeners remember.

Preparation makes everything easier. When you know your message and trust what you bring to the table, you can relax and focus on the conversation. The goal is not to sound perfect. It is to show up as yourself and create a real connection.

As a guest, the interview is your stage. It is your chance to build credibility, communicate what you stand for, and guide listeners toward a next step that feels natural. That might be visiting your website, joining your email list, or booking a call. A strong interview creates momentum that continues working for you long after the episode airs.

Show Up With Confidence and Presence

When you join a podcast, the first few minutes say a lot before you ever get into the real content. Listeners can hear when you are nervous, distracted, or not fully present. They can also hear when you sound relaxed, engaged, and ready for a real conversation. That energy matters more than most people realize.

I learned early on that confidence is not about trying to impress anyone. You do not need the perfect story, a polished script, or a big personality. Hosts and listeners want someone who shows up as themselves and keeps the conversation genuine. That is what builds trust.

This section focuses on presence. It covers simple ways to settle in, calm your nerves, handle small surprises, and start strong. When you feel grounded at the beginning, everything else becomes easier. The conversation flows better, you sound more natural, and you stop overthinking every word.

Putting Yourself Out There

At this point, it is time to put yourself out there. That means showing up with honesty and a willingness to be real. It can feel uncomfortable at first, but the more you do it, the easier it becomes.

I will be real with you. One of my early podcast interviews did not go well. I held back. I was nervous and did not feel like I deserved to be there. Imposter syndrome kicked in hard. My mind kept racing. Why am I even on this podcast talking about SEO and digital marketing? There are so many people more qualified than me. I am not the expert they want.

But I pushed through anyway.

By the end of the interview, the host told me I was one of her favorite guests. I was shocked. I honestly thought it was a disaster. That moment showed me something important. Those negative thoughts were not the truth. They were just noise. And chances are, you will deal with the same thing at some point.

If a host invites you on their show, they believe in your story. They want you there. That alone is reason enough to own your seat at the table.

Once I stopped holding back and allowed myself to open up, everything changed. Interviews became easier. Conversations flowed more naturally. I started connecting with audiences in a deeper and more meaningful way.

You probably will not crush your first few interviews, and that is completely fine. Use them as reps. You are learning how the tech works, how questions are framed, and how to handle curveballs in the moment.

The good news is that most podcasts are not live. If you stumble, you can usually ask for a quick reset or redo. No pressure. Stay present, keep learning, and focus on getting a little better with each appearance.

Managing Nervousness

Feeling nervous before a podcast is completely normal. Most guests feel it. The difference between sounding shaky and sounding confident is not the absence of nerves. It is knowing how to manage them.

Early on, I relied heavily on "fake it until you make it." On the outside, I tried to appear calm and collected. Inside, I was overthinking everything. Every pause. Every word choice. Every possible thing that can go wrong.

What I eventually realized is that podcasts are never perfect, and they are not meant to be. The small imperfections are what make conversations feel human and real. When I went back and listened to my early interviews, I noticed something surprising. The episodes were strong. Listeners enjoyed them. The feedback was positive. I had spent all that time worrying over things no one else even noticed.

With experience, the nerves softened. Not because they disappeared, but because I learned to work with them instead of against them.

Preparation plays a huge role here. When you understand the host, the audience, and the overall flow of the show, you naturally feel more grounded. Preparation creates familiarity, and familiarity reduces uncertainty. That sense of control changes the entire energy of the interview.

Confidence is contagious. When you sound calm and steady, the host relaxes, the conversation opens up, and the audience becomes more receptive. Instead of trying to eliminate nerves, reframe them as energy. That edge can sharpen your focus, add enthusiasm, and help you stay present.

Nervousness never fully goes away, but it does become manageable. With the right mix of preparation, perspective, and experience, you stop fearing it. You learn how to use it.

Handling Unexpected Moments

One of the first podcasts I recorded as a guest took place in the bedroom of my old apartment. I had a roommate at the time and gave him a heads-up that I was about to be on a podcast. I asked him to keep things quiet for the next hour.

About twenty minutes into the interview, we were deep into a conversation when I started to hear a faint humming sound from the living room. It grew louder by the second. I was already a little nervous, and now a full distraction was creeping in.

Right in the middle of answering a question, I paused and said, “I’m sorry about the noise. Can you give me one minute?”

I stepped out of the room and found my roommate vacuuming the floor with headphones on. He had completely forgotten about the interview. I calmly asked him to stop for a bit and explained I was recording. He apologized, shut it off, and that was that.

When I sat back down, I worried the moment had thrown everything off. But the host did not seem concerned at all. She told me this kind of thing happens all the time. Since the episode was not live, she planned to clean up the audio during editing.

We picked up right where we left off.

That experience taught me something important. Unexpected moments are part of podcasting. Tech glitches happen. Background noise happens. What matters is how you handle it. Staying calm, addressing the issue professionally, and moving forward without making it a bigger deal than it needs to be keeps the conversation on track.

Treat every unexpected moment as a brief pause, not a derailment. Most of the time, the audience never even knows anything went wrong.

I Learned This the Hard Way

I was deep in SEO mode, working on backlink research for a client. I was analyzing competitor websites to identify what was working and replicate it. This approach consistently uncovers strong link opportunities, and I was fully locked in.

Then my phone alarm went off. That alarm is my standard ten minute warning before any podcast recording.

I always give myself that buffer to prepare my space, shut down distractions, silence notifications, and close any apps that could interrupt the interview. I have learned that nothing kills momentum faster than a random message popping up mid conversation.

I turned on my lights, plugged in my webcam, and did a quick mic check. Everything looked good. A few minutes later, my second alarm went off. That is my final reminder. I refilled my water bottle and took a quick bathroom break. Small details, but they matter.

I logged into Zoom early, feeling prepared and on time. Then one o'clock came and went. No host.

I waited a minute, then another. At five minutes past, I sent a polite message asking if the interview was still happening. While I waited, I went back to work and spotted a solid backlink opportunity for my client. A competitor had joined a local chamber of commerce and picked up a strong directory link. I started drafting a quick note to flag it.

Then the reply came in. The host was running late and planned to join in about ten minutes.

I responded with "No problem," but internally, I was frustrated.

When the interview finally started, I pushed through and did my best. I answered the questions and provided solid insights. But when I watched the replay later, it was obvious. My energy was off. The frustration showed up in my tone and body language. It was subtle, but it was there. And it changed how the interview came across.

I also noticed something else. I rushed the close. I did not clearly mention my free resource, I did not say my URL slowly, and I skipped the simple next step I wanted listeners to take.

After the episode aired, I checked Google Analytics and saw fewer visits to that page than I normally get from a podcast appearance. That was the turning point for me.

I realized that no matter what happens behind the scenes, delays, tech issues, distractions, the moment the mic goes live, none of that can come with me. As the guest, the spotlight is on you. You set the tone. Your energy shapes how the audience receives your message.

Since then, I treat every podcast appearance like it is live TV. I show up early, stay flexible, and lead with gratitude. Whether it is my first interview of the day or my fifth that week, I bring the same level of focus and professionalism.

Treat every delay as a reset, not a reason to carry frustration into the conversation. It makes a difference. And people can feel it.

Building Credibility and Authenticity

Standing out on a podcast is not about saying something no one has ever heard before. It is about saying something true in a way only you can. What builds credibility is not polish or hype. It is authentic expertise, your perspective, your experience, and the lessons you have earned along the way.

One of the simplest ways to establish that credibility is through stories. Not rehearsed stories. Not perfectly packaged examples. Real moments that show how you think, how you work, and what you have learned. These are the details listeners connect with.

Before an interview, I like to think through a few stories I might share. I do not script them or memorize anything word for word. I keep a short mental list of recent experiences, challenges, or wins that naturally support the conversation. If they come up, great. If they do not, I let them go. Forcing a story where it does not belong always sounds awkward.

Authenticity comes from restraint as much as it does from openness. Knowing when to share, when to listen, and when to let the conversation breathe builds more trust than trying to impress the audience with every answer.

Everything you have learned so far leads to this point. The interview is where preparation, presence, and perspective come together. When you show up grounded and honest, your credibility takes care of itself.

A strong interview does not feel performed. It feels real. And that is what makes it memorable. Credibility is built in moments, not monologues.

Communicate Clearly and Tell Stronger Stories

Once you feel comfortable on the mic, the next challenge is making sure your message actually lands. This is where many guests struggle. They know their topic and have the experience, but the delivery becomes cluttered or overly complex. Listeners will not remember every tactic you share. They remember stories, simple explanations, and moments where something clicks.

You do not need to be a professional speaker to communicate well. Clarity matters more than polish. When you focus on being clear, staying real, and using stories to support your points, people stay engaged. When you speak like a human instead of a lecturer, listeners lean in and trust you more. It took me time to learn this, but once I did, everything changed.

This section focuses on clarity and flow. It breaks down how to shape your answers so they are easy to follow, how to use stories without rambling, and how to communicate in a way that feels natural and engaging. When your message is clear and your stories support it, a good interview turns into one people remember and share.

Clarity creates confidence. When your message is easy to follow, your authority becomes easy to trust.

Effective Communication and Storytelling

Podcasting brings your story to life in a way that is accessible, personal, and built for connection. To reach and resonate with a wide audience, your message needs to feel both timeless and human. Storytelling has always been how people hold attention and create meaning through shared experience.

Strong stories follow a simple narrative. They have a beginning, a point of tension, and a resolution that leaves the listener with clarity or insight. When you can weave your own experiences into that structure naturally, your message becomes easier to follow and harder to forget.

A great story does more than share information. It pulls people in, creates imagery, and takes them somewhere. When done well, your story becomes the emotional center of the interview and the part listeners remember most.

Stories give structure to your message. Structure gives meaning to your words. If listeners can follow your story, they will follow your message.

What Makes a Compelling Narrative?

A compelling narrative draws listeners in and keeps them engaged from start to finish. At its core, it follows a simple structure with a clear beginning, middle, and end. Along the way, it introduces perspective, tension, and resolution. That structure gives your story shape and makes it easier for people to follow.

Depth comes from relatability. When you share real experiences and viewpoints, your message becomes more human. Stories rooted in common emotions like struggle, growth, uncertainty, or progress resonate because listeners can see themselves in them. Just make sure every story goes somewhere. Always bring it back to a resolution so the audience walks away with clarity or insight.

Details matter. Be intentional about what you include and what you leave out. Stick to a consistent tone and theme, and pay attention to pacing so your story flows naturally. Whether your style is lighthearted or serious, commit to it and carry it through the entire conversation.

Delivery matters just as much as content. This is something I have personally struggled with. I tend to speak too quickly, which can make even good ideas sound rushed or unclear.

To fix this, I trained myself to slow down. Before interviews, I place sticky notes on my screen as reminders. One says "Speak slowly" and the other says "Finish every word." These small cues help me pause, enunciate, and stay present while I talk.

A strong narrative is not about saying more. It is about saying the right things clearly, at the right pace, with intention.

If your audience can follow your story without effort, they will stay with you until the end.

Stories

A strong story follows a simple structure. It opens with context, introduces a challenge or moment of tension, moves through a clear arc, and ends with a meaningful resolution. When you start with a personal experience and apply that structure, your message becomes relatable and easy to follow.

The story might come from your business, a challenge you overcame, or a lesson you learned along the way. What matters most is that the listener can see themselves in it.

When I first got into digital marketing in 2007, I struggled to find clients for my new SEO agency. I had no real network and no website. All I had was a Craigslist ad and the hope that someone took a chance on me.

One day, a health insurance agent responded. Instead of offering to pay, he said, "I'll build you a website if you do SEO for me."

At the time, websites were still being built in Dreamweaver using hand coded HTML and CSS. I did not hesitate. He needed leads, and I needed a portfolio. Within a few months, his site was ranking above government listings for competitive insurance keywords. His leads took off.

In return, I finally had a website to promote my own services. But more importantly, I gained clarity. That experience showed me how much I enjoyed this work. Helping businesses grow through digital marketing felt exciting and meaningful. That was the moment I decided to go all in.

This story works because it has a clear beginning, middle, and end. There is a relatable challenge, a simple exchange, and a visible transformation. It also educates without lecturing, which builds credibility naturally.

Use stories like this in your interviews, especially when explaining complex ideas or walking through client journeys. A well told story helps listeners connect with you and remember what you shared long after the episode ends.

If your story has a clear arc and a real outcome, the lesson lands without you needing to explain it. When listeners can see the change, they believe the message.

Anecdote

A full story usually includes an introduction, conflict, climax, and resolution. When one or more of those elements are missing, you are usually telling an anecdote instead. Anecdotes do not follow a strict structure. They focus on a single moment or specific event, often to make a quick point.

One of my new SEO clients was frustrated because their website was stuck on page five of Google and going nowhere. When I looked under the hood, I saw their homepage title tag was literally just the word "Home." That was it.

I updated the title to include a relevant keyword that actually described their business. Within three weeks, they were on page one. Leads started coming in from their website, and they were ecstatic.

That is an anecdote. It is short, specific, and easy to follow. It highlights a common mistake and shows how a small change created a meaningful result. These quick stories add value without slowing down the conversation.

Anecdotes are useful for keeping interviews engaging. You can use them to support smaller points, break down technical ideas, or make otherwise dry concepts feel relatable.

Try to tie your anecdotes to everyday experiences and keep your language concrete. Whether you are sharing a personal moment, a client win, or a quick lesson learned, the key is relevance. If it supports the point you are making, it belongs in the conversation.

Used the right way, anecdotes humanize your message and build trust. They reflect real experience and give listeners something memorable to hold onto. A well placed anecdote strengthens your credibility without sounding rehearsed.

Before each interview, get clear on the main themes you want to cover. Then think of a few quick examples that support those ideas. You may not use all of them, and that is fine. Having them ready makes your answers feel natural and confident.

A good anecdote does not explain the lesson. It shows it. When the example is clear, the point makes itself.

Emotionally Resonant Storytelling

Emotions are what bring stories to life. They give depth to your message and help your audience truly connect with what you are saying. When you tap into emotion, your story becomes more than information. It becomes something people feel.

As you prepare for an interview, think about where emotion naturally shows up in your story. Where might a listener feel surprise, empathy, inspiration, or curiosity? Paying attention to that emotional rise and fall keeps people engaged and makes the conversation more memorable.

One of the most powerful ways to connect is by being open about your struggles. I used to avoid talking about failures in my life and business because I thought it made me look less credible.

After doing dozens of interviews and listening to other guests, I realized the opposite was true. Honesty makes you relatable.

Once I started sharing my mistakes without sugarcoating them, the response changed. Listeners leaned in. The stories resonated more deeply and often turned into lessons others applied. If my missteps help someone move forward faster, that is a win.

You do not have to force emotional moments. Just be honest. Speak from experience. Emotions like hope, fear, joy, and uncertainty are universal. When people recognize themselves in your story, trust builds naturally.

Podcasting today is often visual as well as audio. How you show up matters. Body language, eye contact, posture, and energy all influence how your message is received, even on a remote call.

Nonverbal communication plays a bigger role than most guests realize. Sit up straight. Relax your shoulders. Use natural gestures to emphasize your points. Vary your tone and pace so your delivery feels alive. Expressive delivery, paired with descriptive language, keeps the audience engaged from start to finish.

Your energy, presence, and emotional state shape how your message is received, even when the content itself is strong.

When things go sideways behind the scenes, staying centered becomes even more important. You have to lead with emotion, stay connected to your message, and finish strong. Every interview is an opportunity, and how you make people feel is what they remember most.

Facts inform, but emotion is what people remember. If your audience feels the message, they will trust the messenger.

Structuring Your Response

The easiest way to think about your responses is to treat them like short conversations, not speeches. Every strong response follows a simple flow. You open with clarity, add context, and then bring it home.

Start by making your point clear. If it helps, briefly restate the question in your own words so the audience knows exactly what you are answering. Keep it simple and direct.

Next, add some texture. Share a quick story, client example, or personal experience that makes the idea stick. People remember stories far more than abstract advice.

Then close with intention. Reinforce the main takeaway so listeners walk away with one clear idea they can remember and apply.

This structure is worth practicing ahead of time. Before an interview, take one or two questions you expect to be asked and answer them out loud using this rhythm. Aim for thirty to sixty seconds. If you cannot clearly identify your opening point or your closing takeaway, simplify the answer until you can.

When you repeat this process enough times, it becomes automatic. Your answers sound natural, confident, and easy to follow. Hosts appreciate it. Listeners stay engaged. And your message actually lands.

Answering Questions Clearly and Concisely

One of the most important skills during a podcast interview is listening closely. It sounds obvious, but it is easy to drift when you are thinking about what to say next. Active listening keeps you present and ensures you actually answer the question being asked. If something is unclear, ask the host to repeat or clarify it. Pausing is always better than heading off in the wrong direction.

When you answer, keep it direct. Avoid long tangents or stories that do not clearly relate to the question. Stay focused on the main point you want the listener to remember. Short, clear answers go a long way.

Clarity always beats complexity. Try to avoid jargon or technical language unless you know the audience will understand it. If you need to use industry terms, explain them simply. Your goal is for someone brand new to the topic to follow along without feeling lost.

Here is a simple way to check yourself. If you catch yourself using insider language, translate it on the spot.

For example, if you are a financial advisor, do not say, "We help clients optimize their asset allocation." Say, "We help you choose where your money goes so your risk stays comfortable and your plan stays on track."

If you are a coach, do not say, "I help clients overcome limiting beliefs." Say, "I help you spot the story you keep telling yourself and replace it with a better one you can actually act on."

This translation mindset applies no matter what industry you are in. For example, talking about SEO on podcasts is a good one. Some hosts ask broad questions like "Why is SEO important?" Others jump straight into technical topics like "How do you validate schema markup?" My answers change based on the audience.

Most of the time, I explain SEO in plain language that anyone can understand. Less is more. If you go too deep, you lose people. I keep things simple and use real world examples. If listeners want more detail, I point them to a free resource or my website.

That approach applies to anything you promote during an interview as well. When I mention a lead magnet, I do not over explain it. A lead magnet is simply something you offer for free in exchange for an email address. It brings people into your funnel without pressure. One of my strongest examples is a free list of ChatGPT prompts for SEO. When I tested it against other offers, it consistently outperformed my other freebies.

I learned that by testing everything. I experimented with different topics, layouts, and form designs. One small change made a big difference. Asking for just an email instead of both name and email led to a noticeable increase in signups. Fewer fields create less friction, especially on mobile.

The same principle applies to your answers on a podcast. Cut anything that does not serve the point. If you cannot explain something simply, it is a sign you are saying too much. Before interviews, practice answering common questions out loud in under a minute. If you cannot clearly hear your opening point and your closing takeaway, simplify until you can.

Being concise does not mean holding back on value. It means delivering your message clearly and efficiently so people stay engaged. Brevity is a skill. And the better you get at it, the more your message actually lands.

Handling Tricky Questions

Podcasts are live conversations, and live conversations can be unpredictable. Every now and then, a host will throw a curveball question your way. The key is not to panic. Instead, be ready to guide the moment into something useful and aligned with your message.

Most hosts check in with you before hitting record. They usually ask if there are topics you want to cover and if there is anything you prefer to avoid. Take that moment seriously. Setting boundaries upfront gives you more control and prevents uncomfortable surprises later.

If a subject feels too personal, off brand, or simply irrelevant to the audience, say so ahead of time. You do not owe anyone an on air explanation for why something is off limits. Clear communication before the interview leads to smoother conversations during the interview.

This approach keeps the discussion focused on what matters most to listeners. It also helps the host feel more confident guiding the conversation. Every guest has different comfort levels, and there is nothing wrong with defining yours early.

When a difficult question does come up unexpectedly, pause before responding. Take a breath. You can acknowledge the question and then redirect toward an example, insight, or lesson that serves the audience. Most of the time, how you handle the moment matters more than the question itself.

Being calm, clear, and intentional in these situations builds credibility. It shows you are thoughtful, professional, and in control of your message even when the conversation takes an unexpected turn.

Remain Calm

Tough questions can rattle you, especially when they come out of nowhere. The key is to remain calm. One deep breath can shift the energy of a conversation and give you the clarity you need to respond instead of react.

For me, meditation has been a big help. I will be honest, I am not always consistent with it. A few years ago, a friend gave me a meditation cushion as a birthday gift. I keep it in my office where I can see it every day. Even a short pause to sit on it for a few minutes helps reset my mind and sharpen my focus. I also use meditation apps like Insight Timer, which make it easier to build the habit.

I remember being on a podcast hosted by a crypto expert. Everything was flowing until they asked, "How does blockchain impact SEO?" My stomach dropped. I understood the basics of blockchain, but I had never connected it directly to SEO. For a moment, I froze. Then I took a breath.

I answered honestly and said I was not familiar with the relationship between blockchain and SEO. That honesty gave the host room to reframe the question into something I spoke to confidently. Later, they offered to cut that moment out, but I left the decision up to them. They kept it in, and I was glad they did. It made the conversation feel more authentic.

Moments like this are reminders that you do not need to have every answer. What matters is how you handle the moment.

Staying grounded allows you to respond with clarity and integrity instead of scrambling for something to say.

Before interviews, it helps to have a simple reset habit ready. Use a slow breath, a brief pause, or a mental reminder that you are allowed to think before responding. Practicing this ahead of time makes it easier to stay composed when the pressure is on.

Tough questions will always come up. When you have a way to steady yourself, you can handle them with confidence and keep the conversation moving in a productive direction.

Address Concerns

When a difficult question comes your way, the most important thing is to stay focused on the core message you want to communicate. Take a breath, answer honestly, and do it in a way that feels respectful. The goal is to be real without becoming defensive. A calm, even tone keeps the conversation grounded and productive.

Preparation makes this much easier. Before the interview, spend time getting familiar with the podcast. Listen to a few past episodes, notice the host's style, and pay attention to the types of questions they tend to ask. That context helps you anticipate where sensitive topics might come up and think through how you want to respond.

It is also important to remember that you are allowed to set limits. If there are subjects you prefer not to discuss, bring that up before the recording starts. Clear boundaries upfront prevent awkward moments later and help the host guide the conversation more smoothly.

When concerns do surface during the interview, acknowledge the question and respond in a way that brings the conversation back to value. You can address the issue without going into unnecessary detail or getting pulled off track. Staying focused on what serves the audience keeps your message intact.

Showing up calm, clear, and upfront makes you easier to work with and easier to trust. It keeps the interview flowing while protecting your voice, your boundaries, and the message you came to share.

Redirect

One of the most valuable skills you can develop as a podcast guest is learning how to redirect difficult questions. Instead of getting stuck or defensive, look for ways to guide the moment toward something constructive. A tricky question can become the perfect opening to share a lesson, clarify a misconception, or highlight your experience in a useful way.

Approach difficult questions as teaching moments. When you do, you stay composed and transform potential friction into value. In many cases, these moments end up being some of the most memorable parts of the episode because they show how you think under pressure.

I remember being asked on a podcast about my worst client experience. The question caught me off guard. We have all worked with difficult clients, but turning a podcast interview into a horror story session does not help anyone. I paused, took a breath, and reframed my response.

I said something like, "Every business runs into clients who are harder to work with. That is part of the job. What matters is treating people with respect, managing the relationship professionally, and knowing when it is time to part ways on good terms."

That answer let me stay honest without being negative. It shifted the conversation away from gossip and toward professionalism. And that is the real goal of redirection. It is not about dodging the question. It is about steering the conversation toward something that serves the audience and reinforces your credibility.

When you practice this skill, tough questions stop feeling threatening. They become opportunities to guide the discussion, reinforce your values, and leave a strong impression that reflects well on you long after the interview ends.

Building a Connection With the Host and Audience

A great podcast interview is less about delivering perfect answers and more about building real connections. You want the host to feel like they are having a genuine conversation with you, and you want the audience to feel included in it. That sense of connection is what makes your message stick.

Start with the host. Practice active listening so you are not just waiting for your turn to talk. Show interest in their perspective, respond thoughtfully, and build rapport through curiosity. When the host feels heard and respected, the energy of the entire interview improves.

Then shift your focus to the audience. Make sure every answer serves them through education, inspiration, or insight. Once you understand the question, shape your response to add value and keep listeners engaged.

Whenever possible, speak directly to the audience. A simple phrase like "If you are listening right now" makes people feel like you are talking to them, not just the host. In my experience, leaning into audience engagement has significantly expanded my reach and helped me connect with tens of thousands of listeners.

Do not let the relationship end when the recording stops. Give listeners an easy next step to stay connected, whether that is visiting your website, joining your email list, following you on social media, or accessing a resource created specifically for the show's audience. Clear next steps make the connection feel personal and intentional.

Engagement continues after the episode airs. Encourage listeners to leave feedback, ask questions, or share their thoughts. Simply inviting interaction increases responses. When I directly ask viewers to comment on my content, engagement consistently increases. More engagement leads to more visibility, and more visibility extends the life of your message.

Before each interview, take a moment to identify one question you can ask the host and one way you can directly involve the audience. That small shift changes the interview from a one way conversation into a shared experience.

In short, connect with the host, serve the audience, and invite continued interaction. When you do this consistently, your guest appearances create impact long after the interview is over.

Closing the Interview With Confidence

At some point in every interview, the host will give you space to share what you do. This is where many guests either hesitate or overcorrect and start sounding like a commercial. Neither approach works. The goal is to talk about your work in a way that feels natural, relevant, and aligned with the conversation.

When done well, it never feels pushy. You are simply giving listeners a clear next step if they want to learn more. People appreciate clarity. They want direction, but they do not want to be sold to. Value always comes first.

This section breaks down how to mention your work without forcing it, how to close the conversation in a confident and memorable way, and how to guide listeners toward a next step that feels helpful rather than promotional. When you finish with intention and clarity, you leave a strong impression that carries beyond the episode itself.

Seamless Promotion

The final piece of a strong interview is knowing how to talk about what you do without disrupting the flow of the conversation. The goal is to reference your business, product, or service in a way that feels relevant and organic. When promotion feels forced, listeners tune out. When it feels helpful, they lean in.

Instead of thinking about it as pitching, think about it as building trust. Share your experience, your perspective, and the value you bring. When listeners understand how you help people, curiosity happens naturally. They want to learn more because you earned their interest.

This is where podcasting really shines. You are not chasing attention or convincing anyone in real time. You are attracting the right audience by showing up prepared, confident, and genuine. When you lead with value and clarity, promotion becomes a natural extension of the conversation rather than an interruption.

Keep It Relevant

The most effective way to mention what you do on a podcast is to make it part of the story you are already telling. When it fits naturally into the conversation, it sounds authentic. When it feels forced, listeners can tell immediately. Stories, client wins, and moments from your journey are the easiest way to create that connection.

For example, when I am asked how I got into digital marketing, I share the entire story. I talk about graduating with a degree in Business Marketing, my first job in SEO back in 2007, and how that eventually led me to start my own company, SEO Optimizers. Along the way, I might mention the company name once or twice. That is enough for it to stick without turning the interview into a commercial.

Early on, I did not always get that balance right. There were times when I mentioned my company too often. One host actually stopped me mid interview and said, half joking but serious enough, "That is enough talk about your company. You can promote it at the end." That moment stuck with me.

Since then, I have been much more intentional. If the mention fits, I include it. If it does not, I leave it out. The priority is always to deliver value to the host and their audience. When you focus on helping first, any promotion that follows feels natural and far more effective.

Offer Value

When you talk about what you do, focus less on selling and more on helping. Show listeners how your expertise solves real problems, answers real questions, or makes their lives easier. The more useful you are, the more trust you earn.

Today, I openly share my SEO strategies on podcasts. Early on, I held back, worried about giving away too much. Over time, I learned two important things. Most people listen to learn, not to copy every step. And when you clearly explain how something works, you demonstrate real expertise. That trust is what leads people to reach out.

I went through a similar shift when I started teaching digital marketing classes in 2013. At first, I kept my best strategies close to the vest. The result was predictable. Students felt underwhelmed. Once I started walking through real websites and showing exactly what I do, everything changed. Engagement went up, confidence in my expertise grew, and many of those students later became consulting clients.

Real examples are one of the strongest ways to deliver value. If you can relate your story to clear outcomes, even better. Toward the end of many interviews, hosts will ask about a client success story. That is your opportunity to show proof through experience.

I was recently on a podcast geared toward attorneys who wanted to grow their online presence. When asked for a success story,

I shared how I helped a law firm reach the top of Google Search, Google Maps, and Yelp for their core keywords. I had similar results from a plumber and an ecommerce client, but those examples did not resonate the same way. Matching your example to the audience makes your message land.

This applies in any industry. If you are a health coach speaking to busy parents, share a story about a simple routine that worked in a chaotic schedule. If you are a consultant speaking to founders, share a story about one decision that removed bottlenecks and freed up time.

Lead with value. Use real stories. Tailor your examples to the people listening. When you do that, trust builds naturally and interest follows long after the episode ends.

Call to Action

At the end of most podcast interviews, the host will ask how listeners can find you. Early on, I made the mistake of listing every platform I was on. My website, Facebook, Instagram, LinkedIn, YouTube, and more. It was overwhelming for the audience and stressful for me. Expecting someone to remember even one link is difficult. Asking them to remember several almost guarantees they will remember none.

If your username is consistent across platforms, you can simplify this by saying, "You can find me everywhere at @username." That works well when it is available. In reality, usernames get claimed quickly and platform rules can get in the way. I ran into this myself. My full name was already taken on Instagram, and character limits forced me to shorten it on X. That inconsistency created unnecessary friction.

The solution was to create a single landing page on my website that links out to everything. Now, when a host asks where to find me, I share one simple URL. That small change made a big difference. Podcast appearances started driving steady traffic instead of short spikes, and those visits continued long after episodes were published.

You can take this one step further by offering something valuable specifically for listeners. For example, I send people to a page where they can access a free SEO training, join a private community, or book a strategy session. Giving people a clear benefit tied to one simple link makes it much easier for them to take action.

The key is to keep your call to action natural and useful. Invite listeners to take a next step that fits your business. That might be downloading a free resource, joining your email list, scheduling a consultation, or exploring your product. The goal is not to push. It is to guide interested listeners forward.

Finally, track what happens next. Tools like Google Analytics allow you to see how many people visit your page, where they come from, and what actions they take. That insight helps you refine your approach and make each podcast appearance more effective over time.

Starting and Ending Your Interview Correctly

You've heard the saying that first impressions matter. That is true. In podcasting, your final impression matters just as much. How you open the conversation and how you close it shapes how listeners remember you, how the host feels about the interview, and whether anyone takes action afterward.

A strong opening sets expectations. A strong close creates momentum. When you handle both ends well, the entire conversation feels more polished, purposeful, and memorable.

Create a Hook

Start your interview with something that immediately captures attention. Use a strong statement, an interesting question, or a short story that sparks curiosity. A clear, confident opening sets the tone and keeps listeners engaged from the first minute.

You only have a brief window to earn attention. Show up with energy, even if the recording time is less than ideal or the host is running late. The moment the conversation begins, listeners are deciding whether to lean in or tune out. If you sound distracted or flat, they will move on quickly.

When the host asks, "Tell us a bit about yourself," avoid running through your resume. Job titles rarely connect. Instead, share a short backstory that feels human and relevant to the audience. Focus on how you got here and why it matters to them.

One introduction I often use is how I accidentally got into digital marketing. Back in 2007, I landed a role that involved online marketing even though I had no idea what SEO was at the time. I had no formal training, so I taught myself through blogs, forums, and constant trial and error. That path eventually led me to start my own agency, SEO Optimizers, where I now help businesses grow their online visibility.

That is a hook. It is brief, honest, and easy to remember. It explains who you are, how you got here, and why your perspective is worth listening to, all in under half a minute.

Setting the Tone

Set the tone at the beginning of the interview so it aligns with your core message and carries through to the end. Before you hit record, get clear on the main ideas you want to communicate. That clarity makes it easier to guide the conversation naturally and ensures your key points land by the time the interview wraps up.

Pay attention to the host's style and the overall feel of the show. If the podcast is relaxed and conversational, match that energy. If it is more structured or professional, keep your responses focused and organized. The goal is not to change who you are, but to meet the audience where they already are.

It also helps to acknowledge the listeners early. A simple line like, "I'm excited to dig into this with your audience," immediately shifts the focus outward. It signals that you are there to contribute, not just to talk about yourself. That small moment of awareness sets the tone for a more engaging and collaborative conversation.

Ending on a High Note

How you close an interview matters just as much as how you start. The final moments shape how the conversation is remembered and how you are perceived by both the host and the audience. A brief recap can help, but what really sticks is the energy you leave behind and the intention you bring to the close.

I always make a point to thank the host and show genuine appreciation. There is no need for a script. A simple, sincere thank you goes a long way. Letting the host know you enjoyed the conversation and valued their questions helps end things on a positive note and reinforces professionalism.

When it feels natural, I also mention something specific I appreciated about the discussion or the way the host guided the interview. Thoughtful comments like that are remembered. They signal respect and help strengthen the relationship beyond the episode itself.

Your presence still matters at the very end. Many podcasts are recorded on video as well as audio, which means your posture, focus, and engagement are still being noticed. Staying present and energized through the final minutes, even during a long recording, leaves a lasting impression.

Ending strong does more than create good content. It builds goodwill with the host. Some of my best opportunities have come from staying in touch after an interview. Sometimes that turns into collaborations. Other times it leads to referrals or unexpected partnerships. Those connections add up over time.

After interviews, I like to reflect on how I began and how I finished. Those moments frame the entire episode. I ask myself simple questions. Did I start with clarity? Did I finish with intention? Did my energy feel consistent and genuine? These details often make the biggest difference in how an episode performs and how it is perceived.

Podcasting is not just about reaching new listeners. It is one of the most effective ways to build real relationships. You are spending focused time in a one on one conversation, and that level of attention creates trust. When you finish strong and leave the conversation on a high note, that is what people remember. And in many cases, it opens the door to what comes next.

Quick Closing Checklist

Before the interview wraps up, make sure you:

- Thank the host sincerely for their time and questions
- Highlight one specific moment or insight you enjoyed
- Maintain focused energy through the final minutes
- End with confidence, warmth, and professionalism

Most importantly, remember that podcasting is meant to be enjoyable. Preparation matters, but this is also your space to share your story, your expertise, and your personality. When you enjoy the process, it shows. And that energy is what makes content resonate.

A strong finish is not about saying more. It is about leaving the right impression.

At its core, podcasting is more than promotion. It is storytelling, connection, and contribution. When you finish strong, you are not just ending an interview. You are leaving something meaningful behind.

Why This Matters

A great podcast interview does more than fill time. It builds trust, shapes perception, and creates momentum that lasts long after the episode airs. When you show up prepared, communicate clearly, and close with confidence, you are not just sharing information. You are positioning yourself as someone worth listening to, remembering, and following.

Most guests focus on getting booked. The real leverage comes from how you perform once the mic is live. A strong interview transforms passive listeners into engaged fans and future leads. A weak one fades as soon as it ends. Mastering this part of the process is what separates guests who get results from those who simply show up.

Action Step: Prepare Your Interview Framework

Before your next podcast appearance, create a simple interview framework you can reuse.

Write down:

- One short personal origin story you can use as an intro
- Two to three key points you want listeners to remember
- One relevant example or client story that supports each point
- One clear next step you want listeners to take after the episode

You do not need to script anything. This framework is your anchor. It helps you stay focused, confident, and intentional while still sounding natural and conversational.

When you show up prepared, communicate clearly, and leave a great impression, you have created something valuable. But what happens next is where most guests leave opportunities on the table.

In the next chapter, we will look at how to extend the life of every podcast appearance. You will learn how to turn one conversation into ongoing visibility, relationships, and results instead of letting it fade once the episode airs.

Bonus Resource: Guest Interview Prep Checklist

To help you show up prepared and confident, I created a guest interview prep checklist you can use before every recording. It covers mindset, messaging, delivery, promotion, and closing so nothing gets missed when the pressure is on. This is the same checklist I use before stepping on any podcast.
Access it here:
seooptimizers.com/bonus
Or scan the QR code below for instant access.

PART 3

THE LEVERAGE
(TURNING INTERVIEWS INTO ASSETS)

MAKE THE MOST OF EVERY PODCAST APPEARANCE

Turn every podcast appearance into long-term SEO value, website traffic, and reusable content.

"You don't need more content. You need more mileage from the content you already have."
— Jay Baer

If you're reading this book, you already know the value of landing a podcast interview. It is visibility, authority, relationship building, and credibility wrapped into one opportunity. But here is what most people do not realize. The interview itself is only step one. The real ROI starts after the recording ends.

Over the years, I have been on hundreds of podcasts, and I made a big mistake early on. I treated each interview like a single event. I showed up, did what I thought was a great job, thanked the host, and waited for something magical to happen.

Spoiler alert. Nothing magical happened. No leads. No traffic. Barely any new followers. I started to think podcasting was not working, but the truth was simple. I was not working the podcast.

Everything changed when I shifted my mindset. Instead of seeing each appearance as a one time conversation, I started treating it like an asset I repurpose, promote, and build on. Each episode began generating SEO value, driving traffic to my site, helping me close clients, and opening doors to more podcast opportunities. That is exactly what this chapter is about. Turning one episode into long-term momentum.

This chapter gives you a simple first 48 hours system. These are the moves you make while the episode is fresh, searchable, and easy to share. They are simple steps you can take immediately to maximize the reach of every appearance.

Set Up Alerts So You Never Miss a Live Episode

One of the first lessons I learned as a podcast guest is that not every host tells you when your episode goes live. Some hosts are great about it. They will email you, send a DM, or even share assets to help you promote. Others go quiet. I have had episodes go live three, six, even ten months later with zero warning.

That early window is when you want to be aware and ready to act. If the host does not notify you, it is easy to miss that window entirely.

Here's how I set it up:

- Create an alert for your full name in quotes: "Brandon Leibowitz"
- Create another for your company name in quotes: "SEO Optimizers"
- Choose weekly digest so you don't get bombarded
- Click Save

The quotes matter. Without them, Google will notify you any time someone named Brandon or anyone with the last name Leibowitz appears online. Trust me, you do not want that.

This small step has saved me countless times. I have caught podcast episodes I never knew were published, blog posts quoting me, and even an interview that went live on a platform I had never heard of before. Alerts keep you informed, protect your promotion window, and make sure every appearance gets the visibility it deserves.

Announce Your Episode

Your first step after confirming the episode is live is simple. Make it public. Before you think about clips, repurposing, or long-term strategy, you need to get the episode moving. That first announcement signals to your audience, the host, and the platforms that this episode matters.

Timing is critical. The first day or two after an episode goes live is when it is most shareable, most clickable, and most likely to gain traction. If you wait too long, you lose momentum and visibility that you can never fully recover.

This initial announcement is not about perfection. It is about speed and awareness.

Early on, I made the mistake of waiting too long to announce episodes. I would tell myself I would post later that day or clean up the caption first. By the time I finally shared it, the host had already posted days earlier, the initial engagement was gone, and the momentum had passed. The episode was still live, but the opportunity was not. That taught me a simple lesson. Speed beats polish. The faster you announce, the more reach you capture while attention is still high.

Post a Simple Social Media Announcement

Social media does not need to be complicated at this stage. You are not trying to create a viral post or launch a full campaign. This is your quick breaking news announcement.

When my early podcast episodes went live, I spent way too much time trying to write the perfect caption. I tested different versions, rewrote sentences, worried about hashtags, and overthought the graphic.

Meanwhile, the host had already shared the episode, my audience had no idea it was live, and the ideal promotion window was shrinking. That is when I learned to keep it simple.

Here is the fast formula I use:

- Share the link
- Share a clean screenshot or the cover graphic
- Tag the host and show
- Write one sentence about who the episode can help
- Add one CTA: "Listen here" or "Watch today"

That is it. In less than five minutes, your episode is visible to your audience and to the platform's algorithm. Perfection can come later. For this step, speed wins.

Send a Quick Email Announcement

Social media moves fast, but email sticks. People may scroll past a post, but email lands directly in their inbox. Your message does not need to be long. Think of it as a quick highlight reel.

Email reaches people who already trust you, which makes it one of the highest converting ways to share a new podcast appearance.

Email Your List With a Short Update

I have seen podcast episodes get more traffic from a small email list than from social media posts that reached thousands of people. When you send them something, they pay attention.

Use this simple structure:

Subject:

- New Interview: How to [Main Benefit]

Body:

- One or two sentences on what the episode covers
- A link to listen
- A short call to reply or ask a question

This keeps your audience engaged without overwhelming them. It respects their time while still giving them a clear reason to click and listen.

Share the Episode With Key Contacts

Not every promotion needs to be public. Some of the best engagement comes from private sharing, especially when the episode is genuinely relevant to the person receiving it.

Here is who I share episodes with:

- Past clients
- Referral partners
- Networking connections
- Colleagues who care about the topic
- Anyone in my circle who might benefit
- New leads

One of my longest standing client relationships started with a private message like this. I shared a podcast episode with a former contact because the topic aligned perfectly with a challenge they had mentioned months earlier.

They replied the same day, listened to the episode, and booked a call within the week. No pitch. No follow up sequence. Just relevance at the right moment. That experience completely changed how I think about private sharing. It is not promotion. It is positioning.

Some of my strongest partnerships started because I casually shared a podcast episode at the right moment. Once you have shared the episode on your channels, it is time to bring the host into the promotion loop.

Ask the Host for Easy Amplification

Hosts want their episodes to succeed just as much as you do. Most hosts genuinely appreciate guests who help promote, because it increases downloads, engagement, and overall visibility for the show.

The key is to make promotion easy. Hosts are busy. They are juggling editing, scheduling, and the next round of guests. When you remove friction and make it simple to share, you dramatically increase the chances they will help amplify the episode.

Request a Share or a Post From the Host

You do not need to make this formal or awkward. A quick, friendly message is all it takes.

For example, "Hey, our episode just went live. If you share or tag me, I will reshare everything on my end too." It is casual, respectful, and effective. Many hosts are happy to go a step further once they know you are actively promoting.

They may:

- Share your post
- Send custom graphics
- Provide short clips
- Feature you in their newsletter

Often, hosts are willing to help but will not take action unless you make the first move. Letting them know you are excited to promote removes uncertainty and makes collaboration feel natural. A simple nudge can unlock support that most guests never receive.

Look for Immediate Collaboration Opportunities

The first 48 hours are the best time to strengthen your relationship with the host. The episode is fresh, the energy is high, and both of you are thinking about the conversation, the audience response, and how the episode is performing.

You are not following up out of the blue or trying to restart a conversation weeks later. You are simply continuing a discussion that just happened.

Approach this with a helpful mindset. Instead of asking what the host can do for you, look for small ways you can support their show. When you lead with value, collaboration happens naturally.

These early touchpoints often turn a one time interview into an ongoing relationship. Many of my repeat invitations, referrals, and partnerships started with a simple follow up during this window.

Try these easy collaborations:

- Provide a LinkedIn post they can reuse
- Offer to create a few short clips
- Share a quote they can feature on their site
- Ask if they want a short video teaser
- Write a brief blog summary to help with promotion

These small collaborations give you more visibility while deepening your connection with the host. In many cases, they lead to future invitations, referrals, or partnerships. I have been invited back for second interviews simply because I helped promote and repurpose the first episode more than any guest before me.

Add First Touch SEO Boosts

This is where most podcast guests completely miss out. These small SEO steps take only minutes, but they give each episode long-term visibility.

Embed the Episode on Your Website

When you embed a podcast episode on your site, several things happen at once:

- You give the host an SEO backlink
- You give Google fresh content to index
- You build topical authority
- You create a centralized place for your audience to find interviews

Years ago, I embedded a podcast appearance on my blog and did not think much of it. About a month later, I noticed it was ranking for several long tail keywords related to the topic we discussed. That single embed brought in steady traffic for months.

Here is all you need:

- The podcast player
- One short intro paragraph

- Links to related pages on your website
- A featured image

Simple. Fast. Effective.

Create a Simple Show Notes Page

Your show notes do not need to be complicated.

Include:

- The episode title
- The host name and show
- One short summary paragraph
- Three key takeaways
- Timestamps and or a transcript

This gives Google and AI systems enough context to understand what the episode covers. When you repeat this process across multiple guest appearances, you begin building a powerful SEO footprint that continues working long after the episode is published.

Check Fast Analytics

Do not spend hours analyzing numbers. Just get a pulse and look for quick signals that show how the episode is landing.

Here is what I check:

- Which posts performed best
- What comments people left
- Which topics sparked interest
- What kind of engagement the host received
- Early download or listener numbers

You are not looking for perfection or deep insights yet. You are looking for direction. These signals tell you what resonated and where to focus next.

Identify What to Post Next

Once you have that initial feedback, patterns start to appear. Pay attention to what stands out.

Look for:

- Which topics people reacted to most
- Which quotes grabbed attention
- What questions people asked
- Which moments might make strong clips

This is the bridge between announcing your episode and turning it into ongoing content. Instead of guessing what to post next, you are letting real engagement guide your next moves.

Why This Matters

The difference between guests who get results and guests who do not is not talent or charisma. It is follow through.

The first 48 hours after an episode goes live determine how far it travels, how long it stays visible, and whether it compounds into traffic, authority, and future opportunities. When you have a simple system, you stop guessing and start building momentum with every appearance.

Action Step: Use the 48 Hour Checklist

The next time a podcast episode goes live, follow this checklist within the first 48 hours:

- Post your guest podcast
- Tag the host and the show
- Email your list
- Share privately with key contacts
- Ask the host for a reshare
- Embed the episode on your website
- Create quick show notes

- Check early analytics
- Identify your next content opportunities

Do not strive for perfection. Aim for consistency. Repeat this process for every appearance and your podcasting efforts will begin to compound.

The first 48 hours help you capture momentum, but they are only the beginning. Podcast interviews are not just promotional moments. They are raw material for long-term content.

In the next chapter, we will break down how to turn every podcast appearance into a long-term content engine that fuels visibility, authority, and growth without creating more work.

Bonus Resource: First 48 Hours Podcast Playbook

To help you put this into action faster, I created a podcast promotion checklist you can reuse for every guest appearance. It walks you through the exact first 48 hour actions covered in this chapter so nothing slips through the cracks.

Access it here:

seooptimizers.com/bonus

Or scan the QR code below for instant access.

BUILDING A LONG-TERM CONTENT ENGINE

A podcast interview is not a moment. It is an asset that keeps working for you long after the recording ends.

"Success is the result of small efforts repeated day in and day out."
— Robert Collier

Most people treat podcast guesting like a one time event. You record the interview, share it once, and move on. That mindset wastes the long-term value of every appearance.

When treated as an evergreen asset, a single podcast interview can drive visibility, authority, and organic traffic for years. In this chapter, you will learn how to build a long-term engine that turns each interview into ongoing brand growth.

Host and Organize Your Podcast Content

Podcast hosting platforms make it easy to store and distribute your guest appearances in one place. Even if you have not launched your own show yet, you can upload your interviews and start building a library that grows with every new booking.

I figured this out by accident. At first, I was saving podcast files on my desktop, in Google Drive, and on random hard drives. It quickly became a mess. When a host asked for a clip or a past interview, I had to dig through folders just to track it down.

Once I switched to a hosting platform and put everything into a single, organized feed, everything changed. My interviews were easy to find, simple to share, and ready to publish anywhere with one upload.

That small shift saved time, made me look more professional, and quietly set the foundation for my own podcast.

Podcast Hosting

A hosting platform handles three essential tasks:

- Stores your audio or video files
- Generates an RSS feed
- Distributes your episodes to major listening apps

Instead of uploading your interview to platforms like Apple Podcasts, Spotify, and Amazon Music one at a time, you upload it once and your hosting provider manages distribution across all major listening platforms.

You can begin by publishing your guest appearances as standalone episodes. When you eventually launch your own show, you will already understand how hosting works and have your content organized from day one.

A dedicated hosting feed also makes it easier for listeners to explore your interviews, understand the topics you cover, and follow your appearances across different shows.

Choosing a Hosting Platform

Every hosting platform has different strengths. Some are simple and beginner friendly. Others offer deeper analytics or more advanced features. There is no perfect choice. The right platform is the one you will actually use consistently.

When selecting a podcast hosting platform, look for:

- Straightforward episode organization
- Clear, easy to understand analytics

- Built in distribution to major listening apps
- A clean, mobile friendly player
- Simple playlist or series creation

For my own podcast, I use a hosting platform that keeps episodes organized, makes distribution simple, and provides analytics I actually pay attention to. The best platform is the one that fits your workflow, reduces friction, and keeps your content easy to discover.

The real priority is organization. When your feed is easy to navigate, listeners can quickly find the most relevant interviews. A well structured hosting library improves discoverability and extends the ongoing visibility of every guest appearance.

Turn Your Website Into a Traffic Generator

Your website is one of the easiest places to turn podcast appearances into long-term traffic. When you treat it as a home base instead of an afterthought, every interview can send new visitors, leads, and customers your way for years.

I learned this early. At first, I simply embedded podcast players on a page titled "Podcasts" and moved on. Over time, that page began showing up in search results. Visitors stayed longer. It quietly became one of the highest performing assets on my site.

That was the shift. My website was no longer just hosting content. It was actively working for me.

Website SEO Benefits

Your website is the only place online where you have full control of your content. Social media platforms are crowded and noisy. They are filled with ads, notifications, and constant distractions.

When you host your podcast appearances on your own site, you remove that noise and keep your audience focused on your expertise.

A dedicated page for your interviews helps visitors:

- View your full library of appearances
- Listen without leaving your site
- Learn more about your services
- Take a clear next step through your CTA

I created a central hub for my guest podcast interviews at seooptimizers.com/podcasting, where visitors can explore episodes, listen, and dive deeper into related resources.

How to Build a Podcast Archive Page

A well structured archive page improves the user experience and strengthens your SEO.

Here is a simple layout that works:

- A clear page title such as Guest Podcast Appearances
- A short paragraph explaining what listeners will find
- An organized list of episodes
- An image of the host or show
- A direct link to the full interview
- An embedded audio or video player
- A short summary or key takeaways

This structure makes each appearance easy to access and encourages binge listening.

Why Embedding Works Better Than Linking Out

When you embed your podcast interview on your website, visitors stay with you. When you send them to a third party platform, you give up control of the experience.

Embedding your interviews delivers several benefits:

- Longer time spent on site
- Lower bounce rates
- More internal link clicks
- Stronger engagement signals for SEO

Embedding alone is valuable, but the real SEO lift happens when you expand each appearance into written content.

How to Maximize SEO from Podcast Appearances

Each podcast appearance becomes a standalone blog post. This is one of the most powerful long-term strategies in this entire book.

Search engines cannot fully understand audio or video, but they can read text. A written post gives search engines the context they need to understand, index, and rank your content.

Each blog post includes:

- A short introduction explaining what the episode covers
- An embedded audio or video player
- A transcript or a detailed summary
- Timestamps for key moments
- Keywords pulled directly from the conversation
- Internal links to related pages
- A clear CTA for your lead magnet

On page SEO essentials include:

- Blog and podcast schema
- Proper header structure
- An optimized title tag and meta description

I publish my podcast appearances as blog posts at seooptimizers.com/podcasts. This keeps my blog active with fresh content and creates multiple opportunities to rank for different keywords.

Publishing podcast appearances as both a curated archive and SEO friendly blog posts is a long-term strategy. These assets compound. One interview can continue driving organic traffic for years.

I still receive traffic from interviews recorded more than five years ago because the written posts continue to rank. As long as the content stays evergreen or is updated to remain relevant, there is no reason for it to stop working.

Why Search Behavior Is Changing and Why This Helps You

Search is no longer limited to Google. People now discover content through Instagram, TikTok, YouTube, ChatGPT, Gemini, Perplexity, and countless other platforms. All of them rely on structured information, clear labeling, and written context to understand and surface content.

I started noticing this when people mentioned finding me through summaries, snippets, or AI tools rather than the original episode itself. They had not listened yet. They had read about the conversation first. That shift reinforced why written context matters. The interview opens the door, but the supporting content is what gets discovered.

That is why turning your podcast appearances into keyword rich blog posts creates long-term value. AI tools can process written content far more effectively than audio or video alone. They cannot watch your interviews the way they can read summaries, transcripts, and supporting pages.

When you publish content around each episode, you future proof your visibility and give search engines more ways to surface your expertise.

This is not about chasing new platforms. It is about making sure your expertise can be found wherever people are looking.

Your audience no longer searches in one place. They search everywhere. A long-term content engine works because it meets them wherever discovery happens.

Use Analytics to Improve Over Time

Analytics show you what is actually working so you can improve with every podcast appearance. Most people skip this step, but it is one of the easiest ways to get better results without doing more work.

You do not need advanced dashboards or complicated tools. You just need to notice what stands out.

I learned this after noticing one interview kept driving significantly more traffic than the others. At first, I assumed it was luck. After digging into the data, I realized the host had promoted the episode heavily on LinkedIn and their audience strongly connected with the topic.

That single insight showed me where to double down and which types of shows were worth prioritizing. Once you start reviewing the numbers, even at a basic level, patterns begin to emerge. Those patterns help you refine your message and make each appearance more effective than the last.

Monitoring and Engaging With Analytics

The more interviews you do, the more data you have to guide your future content. Analytics help you identify which shows deliver the most engagement, which topics resonate, and which formats keep listeners interested.

When you understand your numbers, you can make small adjustments that compound over time and ensure every interview performs better than the last. Even small insights add up when you apply them consistently.

Implement Analytics Tools

Most podcast platforms include built in analytics that help you understand how your interviews are performing.

These typically show:

- Total downloads
- Number of plays
- Listening duration
- Audience location

- Device type
- Day by day performance

These metrics reveal clear signals. If listeners drop off early, strengthen your opening. If a specific topic consistently performs well, create more content around it.

Evaluate Listener Engagement

Engagement shows you what listeners care about most.

Pay close attention to:

- Completion rate
- Drop off points
- Clicks to your website
- Social shares
- Comments from listeners
- Messages from new followers

If one interview performs significantly better than the rest, analyze why. Was it the topic, the story, the tone, the host's audience, or the promotional push? Those insights help you make smarter decisions moving forward.

Analyze Demographics and Tailor Future Content

Demographics show you who you are attracting and how different audiences respond to your message.

Common insights include:

- Which age groups engage most
- Which locations drive the strongest response
- Which industries resonate with your story
- How listeners discovered you

Use this data to refine future pitches and topic ideas. When your content aligns with what audiences already respond to, you earn better bookings and build deeper engagement over time.

Your Long-term Content Engine in Action

A well built content engine transforms your guest podcast appearances into long-term assets that continue working for you behind the scenes. Hosting your interviews, optimizing your website for SEO, and reviewing your analytics create a system that grows stronger over time.

Your job is simple. Repeat what works. Adjust what does not. Keep building your archive of interviews and let your long-term content engine compound your authority month after month.

This is how each appearance becomes ongoing visibility instead of a one time spike.

Building a long-term content engine gives your podcast appearances structure and staying power. The next chapter is promotion, so the right people actually see that content and it turns into listens, authority, and leads.

Why This Matters

Podcast guesting only delivers real leverage when it continues working after the interview ends. Without a system, every appearance becomes a short lived spike in attention that quickly fades.

When you treat podcast interviews as long-term assets, you create visibility that compounds. Your content keeps getting discovered, your authority keeps growing, and each interview makes the next one easier to land. This is how guest podcasting turns into a predictable engine instead of a series of one off wins.

Action Step: Turn Podcast Appearances Into Assets

Choose one recent podcast appearance and turn it into a long-term asset.

Create a blog post for that episode with an embedded player, a short written summary, and a clear CTA. Add it to a central podcast archive page on your website. Review basic analytics after it goes live and note what performs best.

Repeat this process for every future appearance.

You now have a system that turns podcast appearances into long-term assets that keep working for you. Your interviews are organized, optimized, and built to compound over time.

The next step is visibility. Even the best content needs distribution to reach the right people. In the next chapter, you will learn how to use social media strategically to extend the reach of every podcast appearance and keep your message circulating long after the episode airs.

Bonus Resource: Podcast Content Engine Checklist

To help you implement this quickly, I have put together templates, checklists, and step by step guides that show you exactly how to turn each podcast appearance into long-term traffic, visibility, and authority.

Access it here:

seooptimizers.com/bonus

Or scan the QR code below for instant access.

PROMOTION STRATEGIES THAT GROW LISTENS AND LEADS

Most podcast guests stop working the moment the recording ends. That is where the real opportunity begins.

"Content is king, but distribution is queen, and she wears the pants."
— Jonathan Perelman

Guest podcasting is only half the strategy. What really drives results is what you do after the interview goes live. Promotion is where appearances turn into traffic, leads, authority, and long-term brand visibility.

Early in my podcasting journey, I recorded a great interview, felt good about the conversation, waited for the episode to go live, and then moved on. I thought the audience would just find it.

That rarely happened. Over time, I learned a hard truth. The guest who promotes gets the most value from the appearance.

Not the guest with the best story. Not the most experienced guest. Not even the most entertaining guest.

Do not just show up. Amplify your episodes and expand your reach with a few simple but powerful promotion strategies. When used correctly, relationship leverage, proof assets, discoverability, and evergreen resurfacing turn each podcast appearance into ongoing visibility and consistent lead flow.

When I promote an interview using the strategies in this chapter, I consistently see 10x more traffic compared to episodes I let sit quietly online. Same host. Same audience. Same content. The only difference is promotion.

Most guests stop too early. This chapter shows you how to keep momentum going. Let's turn your guest appearances into long-term marketing assets.

Follow Up With the Host

Small habits create big opportunities. One of the most impactful things I have ever done in my guest podcasting process takes about 30 seconds. I follow up with the host.

It sounds obvious, but most guests never do it. Once the recording ends, they disappear. Hosts notice that. They may not say it out loud, but they remember who treats the interview like a real collaboration and who treats it like a quick transaction.

I once had a host email me and say, "Brandon, you're the first guest who's ever followed up in a meaningful way. Because of that, I recommended you to three other podcasters who were looking for strong SEO guests."

That single follow up turned into multiple podcast appearances and landed me two clients. Going silent after the recording meant none of that happened.

Another time, I followed up with a host about a release date I had not heard back on. They replied and said, "Oh wow, your episode actually went live two weeks ago. We forgot to announce it."

Without that message, the interview was buried. This is why I set calendar reminders. Relying on memory is risky. Systems do not forget.

Following up has also opened doors beyond podcasts. One message led to a speaking invitation at a virtual marketing summit.

The host told me, "I liked how proactive you were about promoting your episode. We need speakers who do that."

That event drove thousands of views to my content, all from a habit that took seconds to execute.

Build a Spotify Playlist of Your Best Interviews

This is your authority highlight reel. The first time I created a Spotify playlist of all my podcast interviews, I did not think much of it. I uploaded about fifteen episodes, titled it "Brandon Leibowitz SEO Interviews," and shared the link with one potential client.

That link closed the deal. They told me, "I listened to five of your interviews. You clearly know what you're talking about. Let's move forward."

It felt like I had created a digital resume. Only more powerful, because people heard me explain things in real time.

You can apply the same concept to YouTube if your interviews include video. A simple playlist of your guest appearances makes your content easy to binge and positions you as someone who shows up consistently across multiple shows. Some people prefer watching over listening, and YouTube gives those viewers another way to discover and trust you.

Not long after that, a conference organizer messaged me on LinkedIn and said, "I saw your playlist. You've been on a ton of shows. Want to speak at our event?"

A simple playlist opened doors I did not even know existed. Use your playlist everywhere, including your email signature, website, LinkedIn Featured section, when pitching new shows, and when onboarding new clients.

Start with at least ten episodes and add every new one as it goes live. If you do not have ten yet, add what you have and keep building. Something is always better than nothing.

This becomes a trust building asset that works around the clock, even when you are not actively promoting yourself.

Collaborate for Long-term Authority

Collaboration is one of the fastest ways to grow authority without spending money on ads. When you partner with hosts, creators, or peers in your industry, you tap into audiences that already trust them. That trust carries over to you.

I learned this years ago when a podcast host shared my episode with his email list. I expected a few clicks. Instead, my inbox filled up, my social following grew, and people reached out saying they heard me on his show.

That single collaboration outperformed weeks of posting on my own content.

It taught me an important lesson. You can promote yourself all day, but nothing is more powerful than someone else putting their stamp of approval on your work.

When you build the right long-term collaborations, every appearance creates a ripple effect.

Strong collaboration helps you:

- Reach new audiences
- Build lasting relationships
- Strengthen authority through association
- Extend the lifespan of every interview

The strongest collaborations create a mutual promotion loop where both sides benefit. Approach every collaboration as a win win opportunity and invest in relationships, not one time exposure.

Ways to Collaborate with Hosts and Creators

Cross promotion is one of the simplest ways to multiply reach. When a host shares your episode and you do the same, audiences overlap. That overlap builds instant credibility because you are being introduced by someone they already trust.

Ask hosts if they are open to sharing the episode with their email list, posting on social media, or publishing a clip. Offer to match their effort. The strongest collaborations feel balanced and intentional.

Here are collaboration methods that consistently work:

- **Email List Swaps**: Ask the host to share your interview with their subscribers. Offer to promote their content in return.
- **Social Media Cross Promotion**: Coordinate posts so you and the host share the interview at the same time for maximum visibility.
- **Joint Events and Giveaways**: Run a co-branded giveaway, webinar, or live Q and A.
- **Shared Graphics and Video Clips**: Use the same clip or graphic across both platforms. The more consistent the message, the stronger the reach.
- **Trending Topics and Hashtag Alignment**: Tie interviews into trending topics to gain visibility beyond your immediate audience.

Collaboration builds momentum. One strong relationship leads to new listeners, repeat appearances, and opportunities you cannot create on your own.

Treat collaboration as a long-term strategy, not a one time promotion. When you invest in relationships, the results compound long after the episode goes live.

Reinforce Discoverability

Make your interviews easy to find forever. Most podcast guests think their promotion ends after a few posts. That is where momentum quietly dies.

When you build systems that keep resurfacing your best interviews, discovery becomes ongoing instead of temporary.

Here are discovery channels that consistently work well for me:

- **Website**: I maintain a dedicated page that lists every appearance. Some website visitors spend hours clicking through my interviews before ever contacting me.
- **YouTube Playlists**: Some people prefer watching video interviews. A playlist makes your content easy to binge and explore.
- **Lead Magnets**: I add select episode links inside my guides and templates. Readers click them constantly.
- **LinkedIn Featured Section**: This is one of the most underrated discovery tools. One event organizer once told me, "I booked you because I saw your interviews pinned on your LinkedIn."

The Evergreen Promotion Loop

If you only post once and walk away, your content dies quickly. But when you set up a simple evergreen loop, your older interviews keep resurfacing for years. This is my system for getting ongoing visibility without extra work.

Monthly

- Repost one or two high performing clips
- Share a short lesson pulled from a recent episode
- Add one interview to your newsletter

Quarterly

- Highlight your best three interviews
- Swap out your pinned social post
- Add new episodes to your speaker kit

Yearly

- Publish a best episodes of the year roundup

- Refresh your Spotify playlist
- Update your media kit with recent appearances

This system takes very little time because the content is already created. The only work is redistribution.

One episode I reposted nine months later outperformed the original launch week, simply because the right audience saw it at the right time.

Evergreen loops work because most of your audience did not see your content the first time. Or the second. Repetition is not noise. It is how visibility compounds.

Wrap Up

Every interview carries more potential than what happens during the recording. The real leverage comes from what you do next. Promotion, distribution, repurposing, and resurfacing are what turn appearances into lasting assets.

Your podcast appearances begin to compound when you:

- Follow up with the host
- Build your Spotify playlist
- Reinforce long-term discoverability
- Run your evergreen promotion loop

When you do this consistently, visibility increases. Discoverability grows. Credibility follows. You are no longer just a guest showing up for an episode. You are building a brand that compounds every time your voice reaches a new audience.

Why This Matters

Podcast appearances only create leverage when they continue working after the recording ends. Most guests stop too early. They show up, share the episode once, and left it alone. That approach turns powerful interviews into short lived moments instead of long-term assets.

When you follow up, collaborate intentionally, reinforce discoverability, and run simple evergreen promotion loops, each appearance compounds. You stop relying on constant outreach and start building momentum. Over time, your voice reaches more people, your authority grows, and opportunities begin to come to you instead of the other way around. This is how guest podcasting shifts from a one off tactic into a scalable brand building system.

Promotion creates the initial momentum by getting your podcast appearances in front of new audiences. Social media, discussed in the next chapter, is where that momentum multiplies, extending the life of each episode and expanding your reach far beyond the original release.

Action Step: Apply the Full Podcast Promotion Framework

Choose one recent podcast appearance and apply this full promotion framework:

- Follow up with the host and confirm the release and promotion plan
- Add the episode to your Spotify playlist
- Feature it on your website and LinkedIn Featured section
- Share one clip or takeaway instead of posting once and disappearing
- Schedule it into your evergreen promotion loop

Do this for one episode first. Then repeat the process for every future appearance.

Promotion gets people to listen. Systems keep those listens working for you long after the episode goes live.

In the next chapter, we move beyond one time promotion and focus on building a long-term content engine that turns every guest appearance into lasting visibility, traffic, and leads.

Bonus Resource: Podcast Amplification Framework

This downloadable checklist walks you through exactly how to promote each podcast appearance before and after it goes live. It includes follow up prompts, playlist setup reminders, discoverability placements, and a simple monthly, quarterly, and yearly promotion schedule so nothing slips through the cracks. Use it to turn every interview into a long-term asset without adding more work to your week.

Access it here:

seooptimizers.com/bonus

Or scan the QR code below for instant access.

SOCIAL MEDIA STRATEGIES FOR MAXIMUM REACH

Your podcast interview is the spark, but social media is what turns it into lasting reach and real connection.

"Social media is more like a telephone than a television."
— Amy Jo Martin

Social media is one of the most powerful tools you have for promoting your guest podcast appearances. No other channel gives you instant access to a global audience. The challenge is not being on social media. The challenge is using it intentionally to attract, engage, and grow the right audience.

When I started out, I leaned on social media early to build my presence. Over time, that foundation paid off. Today, when I share a new podcast appearance, I expect it to gain traction because I've already done the work to build an engaged audience. It took patience and consistency, but the long-term payoff has been worth it.

Here's how to turn every podcast appearance into a content engine, grow an organic following, and keep your audience engaged without spending money on ads. I've grown my accounts to tens of thousands of organic followers using these exact strategies, and they work when applied consistently.

The key to social media marketing is showing the human side of your brand. People don't connect with logos. They connect with people. When you build that trust, followers turn into fans. Fans don't just watch your content. They share it, talk about it, and help spread your message. That starts with content that actually resonates.

I can post a straightforward video on how to get booked on podcasts and it performs fine. But when I share a real story from my own journey, the challenges I faced, and what I learned along the way, the content lands differently. Stories create connection, and connection drives reach.

That's how you expand your audience while deepening trust with the people already following you. Let's go through a simple system you can use for every single podcast appearance.

Set Up Your Social Media Foundation

It is tempting to try to be everywhere at once. In reality, focus on the platforms where your audience already spends time. Being on every platform might sound impressive, but spreading yourself too thin makes it hard to show up consistently anywhere.

Start by creating accounts on major platforms such as YouTube, Instagram, TikTok, X, LinkedIn, and Facebook. Even if you do not plan to use them all right away, claim your personal name and brand handle before someone else does. Losing control of your handle can confuse your audience and damage credibility if someone else starts posting under your name.

Whenever possible, set these up as business profiles instead of personal accounts. Business profiles unlock features like analytics, scheduling, and performance insights. That data is gold. It helps you understand what is working so you can make smarter decisions and grow faster.

Choose the Right Platforms

From there, decide which platforms to prioritize. You do not need to be active everywhere right away. Focus on two or three core platforms where you can show up consistently and where your audience is already engaged.

If your time is limited, consider working with a virtual assistant and documenting simple standard operating procedures (SOPs) so your content can be repurposed across multiple platforms without extra effort.

One of the best ways to decide where to start is to research your competition. Look them up on major platforms or search their company name in Google to see which social profiles appear first. Pay attention to follower counts, posting frequency, and engagement. Platforms where your competitors see strong interaction are often where your audience is paying attention.

At the same time, do not dismiss a platform just because your competitors are quiet there. They may lack the resources or simply have not figured it out yet. Test it yourself. You might uncover an opportunity others are missing.

It took time for me to figure this out in my own business. Because I work with other businesses, LinkedIn and YouTube became my strongest platforms. Once I systemized my process with SOPs, I was able to repurpose each podcast appearance into multiple pieces of content and distribute it across all my channels.

You have already invested the time to create the content. Make sure it works as hard as possible for you by showing up where your audience actually spends time.

Build a Simple and Professional Profile

Once your accounts are set up, the next step is to make your profiles look credible and consistent. Use a clear, professional profile photo. Write a short bio that explains who you help and how you help them. Add a link to your website, lead magnet, or main call to action. Keep your visual style consistent across platforms so people immediately know they are in the right place.

Next, start spreading the word. Share your social links anywhere your audience already interacts with you, including your website, business cards, email signature, Google Business Profile, Chamber of Commerce listings, YouTube channel, and even during podcast interviews. The more often people see or hear your profiles, the more likely they are to connect with you.

A smart move early on is to claim both your personal name and your company name across all major social platforms, including Instagram, LinkedIn, X, TikTok, YouTube, Facebook, and Pinterest. Ideally, secure your exact name. If that is not available, choose a variation you can use consistently everywhere.

Repeat the same process with your company name so you stay in control of how both you and your brand show up online. As new platforms emerge, claiming your personal and company accounts early helps you avoid confusion and protect your visibility long-term.

Being Social on Social Media

To grow a real following, you need to post and you need to be social. Early social media platforms like MySpace, Facebook, and LinkedIn focused more on networking. Today, most platforms revolve around content. Algorithms surface the posts most likely to keep people scrolling. To stand out, you have to do both. You have to create content and actively engage.

Engaging means liking posts, leaving thoughtful comments, following and subscribing, sending direct messages, and replying to comments on your own content. Posting without engagement might bring occasional reach, but posting combined with consistent engagement accelerates growth and helps you build a loyal, organic following.

One practical way to speed this up is by tapping into audiences who already care about your topic. On platforms like Instagram, X, and TikTok, you can see who follows your competitors. If someone follows your competitors, there is a good chance they will be interested in your content too.

By liking their posts, leaving thoughtful comments, or sending a genuine direct message, you trigger a notification that puts you on their radar. If your content resonates, many of them will check out your profile and follow you.

This is how I have grown my own accounts and my clients' accounts to tens of thousands of real, organic followers. For my business, I engage with followers of other digital marketers. For my skateboarding page, I engage with followers of major skateboarding magazines. The principle is the same. Tap into existing communities and show up with value.

A simple way to start is to spend about thirty minutes engaging with the audience of one competitor. Focus on quality interactions instead of volume. Avoid anything that feels spammy. When done consistently, this approach leads to steady growth in both followers and engagement.

Remember, growth is a balance between posting content that captures attention and engaging with people directly. That leads to the next question. What type of content do you actually post?

Create Content From Your Podcast Interview

When I first started posting on social media, I treated it casually. I shared content when I had time or when inspiration hit. Sometimes a post gets traction. Other times it flopped and I had no idea why.

Eventually, I realized social media rewards consistency and intentionality. When you show up with valuable content on a regular basis, and at the times your audience is most active, growth becomes predictable. Results come from strategy, not luck.

For guest podcasting, that strategy starts with your interviews. Every appearance is a goldmine of content when you know how to use it.

Pull Out Your Best Clips

Think of each podcast episode as one long recording session that can be turned into dozens of short clips.

As you review the interview, look for moments where you:

- Tell a strong story
- Share a specific tip
- Bust a myth
- Answer a common question

These moments make the best hooks. Mark the time stamps during or after the interview, then create short clips around those points.

Short form videos under one minute work best on mobile platforms like TikTok, Instagram Reels, and YouTube Shorts. These need to be vertical so they fill the screen.

Longer clips over one minute tend to perform better on platforms like YouTube and LinkedIn, where people are more willing to watch in depth content, often on desktop or television. Keep those horizontal. Platform preferences change often, so make it a habit to stay current.

The most effective approach is to record once in long form, then repurpose that footage into short clips for faster platforms. AI video editing tools can help with clipping, resizing, and adding captions. Always include headlines and captions so your content grabs attention even when people are watching with the sound off.

How to Turn One Episode Into Endless Content

Repurposing is how you turn one interview into weeks of content. It is the backbone of organic growth because you stretch every episode as far as it can go. Over time, I built simple systems that let me create clips, graphics, audiograms, and short videos without spending hours editing manually.

As you review your interview, note the timestamps where something valuable, funny, surprising, or highly quotable happens. These moments become your clips. A single episode can easily produce 5, 10, or even 20 short videos you can share across multiple platforms.

Tools can make this process faster by handling clipping, captions, and formatting for you. Export both vertical and horizontal versions so your content is ready for every platform. Since most feeds autoplay with the sound off, captions are essential for grabbing attention right away.

Before saving anything, rename your files using clear, descriptive keywords. Instead of "clip1.mp4," use something like "SEO-website-conversion-tips-podcast.mp4." This keeps your library organized and helps your content stay searchable and reusable over time.

I also create a dedicated Google Drive folder for each podcast appearance and store the audio, video, cover art, and finished clips in one place. This makes it easy to scale, delegate, and reuse content later. I focus on creating evergreen clips that can be reposted in the future as long as they continue to deliver value.

Turn Key Moments Into Written Posts

Not every post needs to be a video. You can turn your best moments into short written pieces that highlight your expertise and personality.

You might share:

- A quote from the episode
- A short story you told on the show
- A lesson you shared with the host
- A takeaway that sparked a strong reaction

Pair these with a simple graphic, a still image from the recording, or a branded template from a tool like Canva. Even without design experience, you can create professional looking visuals quickly.

Think of written posts as bite sized extensions of your podcast content. Each post focuses on one clear idea and is easy to scan at a glance.

Turn Your Talking Points Into Carousels

Carousels are multi slide posts that walk the viewer through an idea step by step. They often perform well because they encourage swiping and time on post, both of which platforms reward.

Take one topic from your interview and break it into a simple sequence:

- **Slide one**: hook
- **Slide two**: problem
- **Slide three**: solution
- **Slide four**: example or tip
- **Final slide**: CTA

Once you build a carousel template you can reuse it across multiple episodes. You can apply the same structure on X by starting a thread. Post once, then reply to your own post to continue the idea.

From a single podcast appearance, you can easily pull three strong clips, a few written posts, and at least one carousel. That gives you multiple pieces of content without creating anything new from scratch.

Post With Purpose and Strategy

Once you have content, the next step is to share it in a way that maximizes reach without burning you out. Posting randomly leads to inconsistent results. Posting with a plan creates momentum.

To do that, you need to be intentional about:

- What you post first
- When you post
- How often you post
- How you organize content with a simple calendar
- How you use mentions and hashtags to expand your reach

This framework keeps your content working for you instead of feeling like another task on your to do list.

Decide What to Post First

Lead with your strongest content, not your weakest. The first impression matters, especially when you are introducing yourself to a new audience.

Start with:

- Your most engaging clip
- Your most relatable story
- Your most practical tip

Pair it with a simple caption that thanks the host, mentions the show, and clearly sets expectations for what people will learn when they watch or listen. This gives your content context and makes it easier for new viewers to engage.

Know When to Post

The best time to post depends on your audience's time zone, daily habits, and lifestyle. Instead of chasing generic best times, think about when your audience actually has mental space to scroll, watch, or listen.

A business owner is unlikely to watch a podcast clip at 7 a.m. while rushing to a meeting. They are far more likely to engage mid morning, during lunch, or later in the evening when work slows down.

In my business, Tuesdays through Thursdays tend to perform best. Mondays are often hectic as people catch up from the weekend, Fridays are more distracted, and weekends can be inconsistent depending on the audience.

As a starting point, posting between 9 a.m. and 11 a.m. often works well. You can also test slightly unconventional times, such as 10:37 a.m., to avoid competing with posts scheduled exactly on the hour. Small timing shifts can sometimes help your content stand out.

Use these guidelines as a baseline, then let your analytics guide you. Every audience behaves differently, and your data will show you what actually works.

Know How Often to Post

How often you post depends on the platform and your niche. On some platforms, posting multiple times a day is expected. On others, it can quickly feel like overkill.

For my digital marketing content, I have to be careful not to overwhelm my audience. Most of my followers are busy business owners. They do not want five posts a day about my SEO podcast appearances. A couple of strong posts each week is usually enough.

For my skateboarding page, it is the opposite. The demand for new clips is constant. I can share multiple videos a day and the audience still wants more. Sports, news, comedy, self improvement, and food are other niches where higher posting frequency can work well.

Every audience has a saturation point. The goal is to find the balance between staying visible and becoming noise. A good starting point is one to three posts per week on each platform, then adjusting based on how your audience responds.

If you are unsure, flip the perspective. As a follower of a similar page, how much content makes you start tuning out? Use that as your upper limit.

Use a Simple Content Calendar

A content calendar is simply a schedule that shows what you will post, when it will go live, and where it will appear.

You can start with something as simple as a Google Sheet with columns for:

- Date
- Platform
- Content type
- Topic or hook
- Status

A calendar keeps everything organized and makes it easy to spot gaps in your content. Each row represents one social media post. I like to plan at least a week in advance, and often a month or more.

I schedule clips and posts from my guest podcast appearances once a week, assigning a specific date and time in my calendar. This keeps my social feeds active and consistent, even when I am busy.

Use @Mentions to Multiply Your Reach

Using @mentions is one of the simplest ways to expand your reach without creating any extra content. When you tag the right people, your post is introduced to new audiences who already trust the host or brand you are mentioning.

Whenever I share a clip or post from a podcast appearance, I tag both the host and the show. This links directly to their profiles and notifies them about the post. Many times they will like it, comment on it, or reshare it. One reshare can expose your content to hundreds or even thousands of people who are already aligned with your message.

Tagging only works when it is done correctly. Each platform uses different usernames, and many hosts have similar names, multiple accounts, or separate profiles for themselves and their show. Tagging the wrong account does not just waste the opportunity. It can also look careless.

Before posting, take a moment to double check a few details:

- Confirm the host's correct profile
- Confirm the show's official account
- Mention both in the caption
- Use the show's preferred hashtag if they have one

If you are unsure which account belongs to them, it is better not to tag at all than to tag the wrong person. When done properly, mentions are a free, low effort way to increase visibility, encourage reshares, and build goodwill with podcast hosts and partners.

Accurate tagging allows both of you to tap into each other's audiences, creating more exposure without feeling salesy or forced.

Use #Hashtags to Increase Discoverability

Relevant hashtags can increase the visibility and discoverability of your posts. By placing the number or pound sign (#) before a word or phrase, you turn it into a clickable topic that people can follow.

When I share a podcast episode, I use hashtags related to:

- The podcast name
- The host
- The topic of the conversation
- Broader categories like podcast or interview

I also check which hashtags the host uses and include some of those when they make sense. Aligning your hashtags with theirs helps your content appear in the same conversations and feeds.

Think of hashtags like keywords. Words are joined together without spaces, and longer hashtags are easier to read when you capitalize the first letter of each word.

Avoid overdoing it. A small set of relevant hashtags is usually enough. Adding twenty or thirty to every post can look spammy and, in some cases, reduce reach. The goal is relevance, not volume.

Scale Your Social Media With Systems

Once you have the basics in place, the next step is to save time and scale your efforts with systems. Managing social media manually does not work long-term. The right tools allow you to stay consistent, reduce busywork, and keep your content moving even when you are focused on other priorities.

Use Schedulers to Stay Consistent

Managing multiple social media accounts manually can quickly become overwhelming. Scheduling tools allow you to plan and publish posts across multiple platforms from one dashboard. You do not need every tool on the market. Choose one that fits your workflow, since most offer similar features.

Schedulers make it easy to batch your work. You can sit down once a week, load your posts, choose dates and times, and let the tool handle the rest. Many platforms also offer free native schedulers, such as Meta Business Suite for Facebook and Instagram. TikTok, YouTube, X, LinkedIn, and Pinterest each provide their own scheduling options as well.

I have found that manual posting can sometimes give a small engagement boost because you are present and able to respond quickly. My approach is to post high priority content manually and use schedulers for evergreen or repurposed posts. This balance helps you stay consistent without burning out.

Automate What You Can

In digital marketing, the more you can automate, the more efficient you become. Automation frees you up to focus on strategy, creativity, and growth instead of repetitive tasks that quietly drain your time.

Automation tools connect platforms so they work together automatically. You can set things up so that when you post a podcast clip on Instagram, that same content is published across your website, X, LinkedIn, YouTube, and Facebook. If you are active on multiple platforms, this alone can save a significant amount of time each week.

I also use automation for my blog. When I publish a new post about a podcast appearance, it is automatically shared across my main social channels. Instead of logging into each platform and posting manually, the update goes out everywhere at once, increasing visibility while keeping the process efficient.

Automation is not perfect. Sometimes formatting needs adjusting, a tag does not carry over correctly, or a username differs from platform to platform. In those cases, I step in and make quick fixes. The goal is not to remove yourself from the process, but to reduce friction.

Automation supports your system, not your judgment. When used correctly, it keeps your content moving consistently without burning you out.

Create Simple SOPs for Your Content Engine

An SOP is a step by step guide that explains how to complete a task the right way every time. Think of it like a recipe. Follow the steps and you get consistent results.

For guest podcasting, SOPs ensure every appearance gets the visibility it deserves. Without them, it is easy to forget steps and lose momentum. With them, everything is mapped out, from teaser posts before the interview, to clips after it goes live, to follow up engagement afterward.

The real power of SOPs is consistency and delegation. When everything lives in your head, you become the bottleneck. Once your process is documented, you can hand it to a team member and trust that it will be done correctly. This saves time, keeps your content engine running, and allows you to scale.

You can start simple. A single Google Doc saved in Google Drive is more than enough in the beginning. Create folders and organize SOPs by category, such as social media, podcast promotion, and outreach. As you grow, you can move them into a project management tool if you want more structure, templates, and checklists.

I have systemized my own social media this way, and it has been a game changer. Instead of worrying about every small step, I can focus on higher level growth. SOPs help you move from working in the business to building systems that grow the business.

Grow Your Following Over Time

All of these tools and systems support one goal: steady, sustainable growth.

You grow your following by:

- Posting content that genuinely helps your audience
- Sharing your personality and story
- Engaging with comments and messages
- Showing up consistently over time

There is no instant switch. But once your system is in place, growth becomes predictable. Each podcast appearance feeds your content engine. Each post brings new people into your world. And each new person is a relationship you can build over time.

Repurpose Your Interview Into a Content Machine

Whenever I'm on a podcast, I'm not just thinking about the interview itself. I'm also thinking about the content machine built into it.

One interview can create:

- Dozens of clips
- Multiple quote graphics
- Carousels
- Reels
- Blog posts
- Short tutorials
- Email stories
- Lead magnet content

I didn't always approach podcasting this way. In the beginning, I reposted the full episode and did nothing else. Once I started clipping my strongest moments, everything changed. My social engagement increased almost immediately.

One time, I clipped a moment where I explained how to analyze your competitors' keywords without digging into website code. That clip went viral on YouTube Shorts, reached thousands of viewers, and brought in more leads than the full podcast episode ever did.

The host even messaged me afterward and said, "Your clip is bringing listeners back to the full episode. Keep posting them." That experience reinforced something important. Repurposing multiplies your reach in ways you cannot predict.

Identify Key Moments

Look for moments where you:

- Break down a concept simply
- Share a personal story
- Give a tactical step
- Drop a surprising insight
- Make the host laugh
- React naturally to a question

These moments draw people in and feel authentic on social media. One guest interview of mine produced 18 usable clips. I didn't plan for that. I found them by watching the recording with fresh eyes.

Clip the Content

If the host provides assets, use them. Many hosts send pre edited vertical clips, thumbnails, or cover art. Still, do not rely solely on the host. If I want specific clips or formats, I create them myself.

One tip I wish I had learned sooner is to record interviews in both horizontal and vertical formats whenever possible. This makes repurposing much easier. If you are only filming horizontally, leave space on the left and right so the footage can be cropped cleanly for vertical clips without cutting off important visuals.

Share the Content (But Not All at Once)

I made this mistake early on. I released everything in a single day and then shifted my focus elsewhere.

The problem is that algorithms do not reward content bursts. They favor consistency over one time floods.

Instead of dumping everything at once, I now spread my content out across all my channels:

- Instagram
- LinkedIn
- YouTube
- TikTok
- X
- Facebook
- My email list
- My website
- My speaker page

I also repost winning clips over time. A clip that flopped in May might perform extremely well in November. Timing matters, and consistent distribution gives your content more chances to succeed.

Why This Matters

Guest podcasting does not end when the interview is over. The real leverage comes from what you do next.

When you follow a clear social media system, every podcast appearance works harder for you. Instead of a single spike in attention, you create ongoing visibility, repeat exposure, and new entry points for people to discover your brand. Over time, this compounds. One interview turns into dozens of touchpoints across platforms, and those touchpoints turn into relationships, subscribers, and leads.

Here is the simple playbook you can use for every guest podcast appearance:

- Claim your personal and company handles on all major platforms
- Choose two or three primary platforms to focus on
- Optimize your profiles so they look professional and clear
- Engage with followers of competitors and related accounts
- Pull multiple clips, quotes, and ideas from each interview

- Create a mix of videos, graphics, written posts, and carousels
- Plan at least one week of posts at a time
- Tag the host, tag the show, and use a handful of relevant hashtags
- Use schedulers, automation tools, and SOPs to save time
- Keep showing up consistently and let the system compound over time

When this process is in place, promotion stops feeling overwhelming and starts feeling repeatable.

Action Step: Turn One Podcast Into a Week of Content

Take one recent or upcoming podcast appearance and map out one full week of social media promotion.

Decide:

- Which clip you will post first
- Which quote or lesson you will share
- Which day and time each post will go live
- Which host and show accounts you will tag
- Which three to five hashtags you will use

Add everything to your content calendar and schedule as much as possible in advance. The goal is not perfection. The goal is consistency.

Social media expands your reach, but it is still rented attention. Algorithms change and reach fluctuates. To build long-term stability, you need a direct line to your audience that you control. In the next chapter, we will look at how email marketing gives you that control.

Bonus Resource: Podcast Content Repurposing Checklist

To help you stay organized and consistent, I created a simple checklist you can use for every guest podcast appearance. It walks you through pulling clips, creating posts, organizing assets, and scheduling content so nothing slips through the cracks. This is the same framework I use to transform one interview into weeks of content.

Access it here:

seooptimizers.com/bonus

Or scan the QR code below for instant access.

EMAIL MARKETING AND AUDIENCE GROWTH

Email marketing turns one podcast appearance into an ongoing relationship with an audience that wants more from you.

"Email is still the most personal way to reach people at scale."
— Ann Handley

Email marketing remains one of the most effective digital marketing strategies, especially when it comes to amplifying guest podcast appearances. It allows you to extend the life of every interview and turn short term attention into long-term engagement. That is why this chapter exists. To share what has worked for me and how you can apply it to your own promotion strategy.

Email campaigns help you leverage your existing subscriber base by keeping people informed, engaged, and connected to your content. Whenever I send an email about a recent guest podcast episode, I see an immediate lift in engagement. When I share a YouTube video with my email list, it often results in a noticeable spike in views, likes, comments, and even new subscribers shortly after the send.

The difference between an interview that gets heard once and one that continues working for you long after it airs is what you do next.

Choose the Right Email Platform

To run effective email campaigns, you need an email marketing platform to keep everything organized. While it is technically possible to send emails manually, doing so is time consuming, prone to errors, and nearly impossible to scale. The last thing you want is to accidentally send the same email twice about a podcast interview. That is a fast track to unsubscribers.

These platforms save a significant amount of time and make your outreach feel more professional. There are dozens of other tools on the market, with new platforms launching regularly, especially those powered by AI. While most are not free, your time is valuable. These tools pay for themselves by helping you work more efficiently and focus on higher value parts of your business.

If you are just getting started and your budget is tight, some platforms offer free plans for a limited number of subscribers. That is not ideal for long-term growth, but it can be enough to help you get your email marketing system up and running.

When choosing a platform, look for features that support guest podcast promotion:

- Automations to schedule follow ups or welcome new subscribers
- A/B testing to refine subject lines and content
- Audience segmentation to target specific groups
- Personalization to increase engagement
- Analytics to track what is working
- Integrations with other tools you already use

You do not need the perfect platform. You just need one that you will actually use. Once your system is in place, the most important work begins. Building a list of people who genuinely want to hear from you.

Build a List From Your Podcast Appearances

The hardest part of email marketing is building your list. Asking someone for their email is asking for access to a crowded inbox. People do not give that access away casually. You have to earn it.

There are many ways to collect email addresses, but not all of them work well. Back in 2007, I simply asked website visitors to sign up for my newsletter. That approach brought in a few signups here and there, but in reality, it failed. An email address is personal. People will not hand it over without a clear reason. Trust and value come first.

Today, I rely heavily on lead magnets. A lead magnet is a free offer that provides real value in exchange for an email address. Think of it as a bridge between attention and relationship building. When done right, it pulls people into your ecosystem instead of pushing messages at them.

Common lead magnets include:

- Ebooks or guides
- Checklists or templates
- Webinars or workshops
- Discounts or free trials
- Exclusive or early access to content

The more value your offer provides, the stronger your conversion rate will be. In rare cases where the offer, audience, and timing are perfectly aligned, I have seen lead magnets convert as high as 75%. That level of performance is atypical and not a benchmark. What matters far more than raw numbers is relevance.

Relevance is especially important with guest podcasting. When someone hears you on a podcast and immediately sees an offer that connects directly to what you discussed, conversion rates tend to outperform standard traffic sources.

For podcast appearances, strong lead magnet ideas include:

- Special access to extended or bonus interviews
- Unreleased content that did not make it into the episode
- Early access to upcoming interviews or resources
- Summaries of your interviews with clear action steps

One example comes from a podcast interview where I explained different ways to find keywords. During that conversation, I covered how to search Google and analyze the blue clickable links competitors use, pull keyword ideas directly from competitor sites, and use Google Keyword Planner to check monthly search volume and identify strong opportunities.

I turned that material into a simple PDF and offered it as a lead magnet. That single resource continues to bring in subscribers years later because it solves a specific problem for a specific audience.

Once you have a lead magnet, you need a landing page to promote it. Design matters, but clarity and conversion matter more. A strong landing page clearly communicates value and removes friction.

Focus on these core elements:

- Headline that states the value clearly and makes a promise
- Benefits that emphasize outcomes rather than features
- Clear and concise copy that respects short attention spans
- Trust signals such as testimonials or social proof, when available
- Focused layout without unnecessary navigation or distractions
- A call to action that stands out and uses clear, compelling language

One important caveat. Never buy an email list. Purchased lists are usually recycled and overused. Sending to them is essentially spam. It damages deliverability, hurts your reputation, and can create long-term problems for your business. Ten engaged subscribers who know you and trust you are far more valuable than thousands of people who have never heard of you.

Building a strong list takes time, but it is one of the best investments you can make. When you treat your subscribers with respect and consistently deliver real value, your email list becomes one of the most powerful assets you own.

Segment Your Audience The Smart Way

Once you start building your list, the next step is segmentation. Segmentation simply means dividing your subscribers into groups so you can send more relevant messages.

Without segmentation, everyone receives the same email. That usually leads to lower open rates, fewer clicks, and more unsubscribes. With segmentation, you can send the right message to the right person at the right time, which is where email starts to work in your favor.

When I appear as a guest on podcasts, I often offer a free gift near the end of the interview. When listeners claim that gift, they provide their name and email address and are added to my list. That part is straightforward. The real leverage comes from what happens next.

When someone signs up for a specific gift, I immediately tag them based on that topic. The tag tells my system what they are interested in and how they found me. After they opt in, they receive the promised resource by email. A few days later, I follow up with a link to a page on my site that highlights my guest podcast appearance.

From there, I continue sending content related to the topic they originally requested. I am not pushing a sale or rushing them toward an offer. I am building trust, reinforcing expertise, and staying relevant to what they already told me they care about.

There are many ways to segment your subscribers, but you do not need to overcomplicate it.

Common segmentation approaches include:

- By interest, based on the lead magnet or topic they requested

- By behavior, such as links they clicked or actions they took
- By demographics, including location, role, or industry
- By engagement, separating highly engaged readers from those who have gone quiet

Start by thinking about how someone joined your list and what problem they were trying to solve. Tag them in a way that makes sense for your business, then use your analytics to see which segments respond best over time. As your messaging becomes more specific, your emails will feel less like broadcasts and more like conversations, which is exactly what your audience wants.

Write Emails People Actually Want To Read

Email works when each part does its job. The subject line earns the open. The preview text reinforces that decision. The email body delivers value and guides the reader toward action. When these elements work together, your emails feel intentional, relevant, and worth reading.

You can write the most thoughtful email in the world, but without a strong subject line, it will never get opened. In email marketing, the subject line is your first impression. It determines whether your message gets opened, ignored, deleted, or flagged as junk before the reader ever sees your content.

Subject Lines That Get Clicks

Your subject line is the single biggest factor in whether your email gets opened. If it misses, nothing else matters. A strong subject line earns attention and sets expectations without feeling pushy or misleading.

Effective subject lines tend to share a few traits:

- Stay short, ideally under 50 characters, so they do not get cut off on mobile

- Lead with curiosity or a clear benefit
- Occasionally include the subscriber's first name
- Stand out in a crowded inbox without sounding spammy

I regularly test subject lines to see what performs best. On my list, subject lines that highlight the benefit of a podcast interview consistently outperform simple episode titles. Mentioning words like podcast or video replay early in the subject line also tends to improve open rates because it clearly signals what the email contains.

As a general benchmark, a healthy open rate is around 35%, with a minimum target of roughly 25%. These numbers will vary by industry and audience, but they give you a useful baseline.

If your open rates consistently fall below that range, start by testing new subject lines. You can also clean inactive subscribers from your list and review deliverability settings to make sure your emails are actually reaching inboxes.

Here are a few subject line examples you can adapt for your own podcast promotion:

- Exclusive. My deep dive into [topic]
- Just released. My guest interview on [podcast name]
- I shared everything about [topic] in this interview
- Here is the replay from my latest podcast appearance

The goal is not to be clever. The goal is to be clear, relevant, and compelling enough that the right people want to open and read what you sent.

Preview Text That Supports the Subject

Preview text appears next to the subject line and gives readers one more reason to open your email. Think of it as a continuation of the subject, not a summary of the email. Try to keep it under 40 characters so it does not get cut off on mobile devices.

When your subject line and preview text work together, they create curiosity while setting clear expectations for what's inside.

Email Body That Delivers Real Value

Once someone opens your email, you need to hook them quickly. The first sentence matters because many email clients display it as the inbox preview when no preview text is added.

You can open with a question, a surprising insight, or a clear statement of value. For example, "Many podcast listeners say they are more likely to trust a brand or expert they hear on a podcast." A line like this immediately frames the email and gives the reader a reason to keep going.

The goal of your email body is not to say everything. It is to deliver value, build interest, and guide the reader toward a single next step.

Keep these best practices in mind as you write:

- **Keep it brief and valuable.** Highlight one or two key takeaways from your guest podcast appearance. Focus on what the reader will learn or gain, not on recapping the entire conversation.
- **Use readable font sizes.** I write in 14 point font because most people read email on their phone. If your audience skews older, 16 point can work even better. Anything smaller than 14 point is difficult to read on mobile.
- **Break up the text.** Limit paragraphs to two or three sentences. Single sentence paragraphs are effective and easier to scan. Avoid large blocks of text that feel heavy or overwhelming.
- **Use visuals carefully.** Images and videos can affect deliverability and are often blocked by email clients. Start with text first, then test visuals to see how your audience responds.
- **Build anticipation.** Tease a compelling insight or highlight from your interview to spark curiosity and encourage clicks before or after the episode goes live.

When your email body respects the reader's time and delivers real value, it feels helpful instead of promotional. That is what keeps people opening your emails and looking forward to the next one.

Calls To Action That Get Clicks

Every email needs to have one clear call to action. Not three. Not five. One specific next step you want the reader to take.

Too many options create decision fatigue. Think of a restaurant with a menu that is ten pages long. People freeze, make a random choice, or walk away altogether. The same thing happens in email. When readers are unsure what to do next, they often do nothing.

For podcast promotion, your primary call to action is usually one of the following:

- Listen to the full episode
- Watch the video replay
- Download a related resource

Make your call to action easy to see and easy to click. A button works well, but a clear text link can be just as effective. What matters most is clarity. The reader never has to guess what happens when they click.

One simple tactic that often gets overlooked is adding a short P.S. line at the end of your email. Many people skim the subject line and opening sentence, then jump straight to the P.S. Use that space to restate your main call to action in a natural, low pressure way.

For example, "P.S. If you missed my latest podcast interview on [podcast name], you can listen to it here." This kind of reminder feels helpful rather than pushy, but it still nudges the reader toward taking action.

Optimize Timing and Personalization

Even the best email can fall flat if it arrives at the wrong time or feels like it was written for everyone instead of someone.

Email works a lot like social media. You can have a strong subject line and a solid message, but if your email lands in the inbox when your audience is busy, distracted, or offline, it gets buried. Timing determines whether your message gets seen. Personalization determines whether the reader cares enough to open it and engage.

When you get both right, your emails stop feeling like broadcasts and start feeling like conversations. That shift is what turns occasional opens into consistent engagement.

Find Your Best Send Times

There is no universal perfect send time, but there are reliable starting points. For many audiences, emails sent Tuesday through Thursday in the mid morning tend to perform well. That said, every list behaves differently, which is why testing matters.

To identify what works best for your audience, start simple. Begin with common weekday windows, then send the same email at different times to different segments. Watch your open and click rates closely and look for patterns. Once you see certain days or times consistently outperform others, lean into those windows.

Think of timing as another lever you can pull to improve results. Small adjustments can lead to noticeable gains in visibility, engagement, and clicks.

Use Personalization To Stand Out

Personalization is one of the simplest ways to improve email performance. When you collect a subscriber's first name, you can use it in subject lines and body copy to make your emails feel more direct and intentional.

Keep your lead magnet opt in forms simple. Ask for a first name and an email address. The fewer fields you require, the more people will complete the form. You can always gather additional details later as the relationship develops.

For example, subject lines like, "John, here is my latest podcast interview on [topic]" often outperform versions that do not include a name.

The same applies to opening lines. Using a subscriber's name early, such as, "Sarah, I just shared this on a podcast, and I think you will find it helpful," helps establish a more personal connection and builds trust.

People respond to personalization because it signals that you are speaking directly to them, not sending another generic broadcast. You can test this by comparing emails that include names with those that do not. Pay attention to how personalization impacts open rates, clicks, and unsubscribes so you can refine what works best for your audience.

Use Testing and Analytics To Improve Results

If you are not testing, you are leaving money on the table. Small changes can make a significant difference in performance. Subject lines, email layout, personalization, and send times all influence conversions.

Start With Simple A/B Tests

A/B testing means creating two versions of the same email. One portion of your list receives version A and the other receives version B. By comparing performance, you can see which version drives better results. Your email platform analytics provide the data you need to make informed decisions instead of guessing.

The best place to start is with small, high impact tests. Focus on one variable at a time so you know exactly what influenced the outcome.

Strong testing areas include:

- **Subject lines**. This is the most effective place to test. Try reordering words, adding personalization, changing tone, or experimenting with different hooks.
- **Send times and days**. After subject lines, test when your emails are delivered to see when your audience is most engaged.
- **Email body**. Test length, structure, and formatting. Compare short versus long form content and experiment with spacing and layout.
- **Offers**. Test how you frame your call to action. Even small wording changes can affect conversion rates.

One way I generate testing ideas is by subscribing to a variety of marketing email lists using an old email address. Once a week, I skim those emails and note subject lines or formats that stand out. I do not copy them, but I adapt ideas that feel relevant to my audience and goals.

Testing is ongoing. When you find a winner, test it against a new variation. If a test underperforms, revert to what worked before and try a different approach. Over time, these small optimizations compound and lead to stronger, more consistent results.

Use Analytics To Guide Your Decisions

Analytics show you what is actually happening with your emails. Instead of guessing, you can look at the data and see which campaigns worked, which ones underperformed, and where to make adjustments. The metrics that matter most are tied to deliverability, engagement, list health, and conversions.

Most email platforms provide a similar set of core metrics, including:

- **Open rate.** How many people opened your email.
- **Click through rate.** How many people clicked a link inside the email.
- **Click to open rate.** Of the people who opened the email, how many actually clicked.
- **Bounce rate.** The percentage of emails that were not delivered.
- **Unsubscribes.** How many people opted out after receiving the email.
- **Spam complaints.** How often emails were flagged as spam.
- **Conversion rate.** How many people took the action you wanted, such as watching your podcast or signing up for a resource.

Rather than obsessing over a single campaign, look for patterns over time. Is your open rate trending up or down? Are clicks increasing as you refine your messaging? Do unsubscribes spike after certain types of emails? Those trends are far more valuable than any one data point and will guide smarter decisions going forward.

It is also important to remember that email is usually just one step in a larger journey. Add UTM tracking to your links so you can see what happens after someone clicks. Did they listen to your podcast, visit your site, or complete a conversion? Connecting email data with analytics tools gives you a clearer picture of how your campaigns contribute to real outcomes.

Analytics are not just numbers on a dashboard. They are feedback from your audience. They show you what resonates, what gets ignored, and what motivates people to take action. Use that feedback to refine your subject lines, test new approaches, and improve each campaign over time. Small insights, applied consistently, lead to meaningful gains.

Integrate Email With The Rest Of Your Marketing

Connecting your email platform with the rest of your marketing tools saves time, reduces errors, and keeps your systems running smoothly. Integrations handle repetitive tasks automatically and ensure your data flows where it needs to go without manual effort.

Manually adding new subscribers to your email list is inefficient and frustrating. It slows you down, introduces delays, and creates a poor experience for people who expect instant access after signing up. With integrations in place, subscribers are added automatically and receive the right emails immediately.

Here is how I use integrations in practice. After a guest podcast appearance, I send listeners to a gift landing page where I offer a replay of one of my digital marketing seminars. When someone signs up, they expect to receive the details right away. That happens automatically because the landing page form is connected to my email platform. There is no copying and pasting, no waiting, and no room for error. Everything works in real time.

You can set this up directly inside your email provider or use an automation tool like to connect different systems. The specific tool matters less than the experience. From the subscriber's perspective, the process feels seamless. Even a short delay can make your brand feel disorganized and can cost you leads.

Once your core integrations are in place, you can automate more advanced workflows, such as automatically tagging subscribers based on the page or form they used, adding new contacts to specific email sequences, notifying yourself or your team when someone completes an important action, or syncing subscriber data with your CRM or booking system.

These connections reduce manual work and eliminate busywork. More importantly, they free up time and mental energy so you can focus on higher value activities like booking more podcast appearances, creating better content, and serving your clients.

As you review your current setup, look for one place where manual work can be removed. Connecting your main lead magnet form to your email platform so new subscribers instantly receive a welcome email and the promised resource is a strong place to start.

Why This Matters

Guest podcast appearances create attention, but attention alone does not build a business. Without a system to capture and nurture that interest, most listeners will hear you once and disappear.

Email marketing is what turns one time listeners into long-term subscribers, repeat visitors, and future clients. It gives you a direct line to people who already trust your voice and want to hear from you again.

When done correctly, every podcast interview becomes more than content. It becomes the start of a relationship that compounds over time. This is how you make your podcast appearances work long after the episode airs.

Action Plan: Your Email Growth

Use this playbook to turn podcast listeners into subscribers and fans:

- Choose one email platform and set up your list
- Create one simple lead magnet tied to your podcast content
- Build a landing page and connect it to your email tool
- Start collecting emails from your podcast appearances and website
- Segment your audience based on interests and behavior
- Write subject lines that highlight the value of your interviews
- Keep your emails clear, personal, and focused on one main call to action
- Test send times, subject lines, and formats

- Watch your analytics and adjust based on what your audience responds to
- Use integrations and automations so your system runs consistently

You do not need to do everything at once. Start with one step, get it working, then layer in the rest.

Email marketing helps you nurture relationships and turn listeners into long-term subscribers.

But even with strong follow up systems in place, small mistakes can quietly cost you podcast bookings before the opportunity ever starts. In the next chapter, we will break down the most common rookie mistakes that stop guests from getting booked and how to avoid them.

Bonus Resource: Email Growth Action Plan

If you want a clear system to follow, I created a downloadable checklist that walks you through the entire process step by step. You can use it whether you are starting fresh or refining what you already have in place.

Access it here:

seooptimizers.com/bonus

Or scan the QR code below for instant access.

PART 4

THE EVOLUTION
(BUILDING LONG-TERM AUTHORITY)

ROOKIE MISTAKES THAT COST YOU BOOKINGS

Avoid the most common podcast guest blunders I've seen and made so you don't lose your shot before it even starts.

"The best way to predict the future is to create it."
— Peter Drucker

Every new podcast guest makes mistakes in the beginning. That is part of the process. The good news is that most rookie slip ups are completely avoidable once you know what to look for. This final chapter walks you through the most common errors that can cost you bookings and credibility, along with simple ways to avoid them.

As you continue your podcasting journey, keep an eye on seven predictable pitfalls. Lack of preparation, forced self promotion, and ignoring the host's style can turn listeners away fast. Losing track of your key messages, overlooking the technical setup, or stretching the interview past the agreed time can also weaken your impact. One of the biggest missed opportunities is forgetting to deliver a clear CTA or failing to follow up with the host after the interview.

What follows is a practical guide to help you avoid these mistakes and show up as a confident, prepared, and memorable guest every time.

Inadequate Preparation

Inadequate preparation is the most common mistake new podcast guests make. Many beginners think they can improvise the entire conversation or rely on natural charisma. That approach usually backfires.

Early in my podcasting journey, I joined a show without researching the host or the format. I figured it was a standard interview where I answered questions and shared a few stories. Instead, the host put me in a five minute hot seat and asked me to deliver five rapid fire tips, with no warm up and no guiding questions.

I managed to wing it, but it was stressful, and I delivered far more value once I started taking ten minutes to understand the structure ahead of time. After that experience, I never arrived unprepared again.

A lack of preparation can lead to awkward answers, missed points, or moments where you talk past the host or the audience. None of that helps your credibility. The easiest way to prevent these situations is to show up informed.

Research the podcast and get a feel for its tone and audience. Map out your core points and the examples you want to share. Think through the questions you expect and how you want your answers to land.

Excessive and Unnatural Self-Promotion

Another rookie mistake is going too hard on self promotion. I get it. You want people to know who you are and what you do. That is part of why you are on the podcast in the first place. The problem is that listeners can tell when the conversation turns into a sales pitch, and they check out fast.

I did this often when I first started. I kept mentioning my company at the beginning of interviews because I thought it made me sound more credible. It did the opposite. It felt forced and a little awkward.

Most hosts give you space at the end to promote yourself without holding back. Once I learned to wait for that moment, everything flowed better. The hosts appreciated it, and the audience stayed engaged.

The key is to focus on value first. Share something useful. Tell a story. Walk listeners through a tip they can try today. Then, if it fits naturally, mention your business or a resource you offer.

When you lead with helping instead of selling, people trust you more and your promotional moments land the right way.

How to Adapt to Each Show's Format and Style

Every podcast has its own rhythm. Some shows are structured and serious. Others are loose, funny, and built around banter. If you show up the same way on every podcast, you will miss the mark more often than you realize.

When I started guesting, I expected my regular style to work everywhere. It did not. I ended up on a show that leaned heavily into jokes and playful back and forth. I came in too formal at first, and it took me a few minutes to loosen up. Experiences like that taught me how important it is to match the tone of the host and the audience.

You will start to notice these differences when you research shows. One podcast might want deep technical advice for industry insiders. Another might focus more on stories, personality, and spontaneous conversation. You want to be able to shift between both. The more flexible you are, the better the interview will land.

The easiest way to avoid this mistake is to listen to a few recent episodes before you go on. Pay attention to the pace, how the host asks questions, and how guests respond. During the interview, stay aware of the host's cues. If they joke, joke back. If they move into a more serious lane, follow them there. When you adjust in real time, the conversation feels natural and the audience stays engaged.

Failure to Stick to Key Messages

Listeners can tell when a guest starts to drift. A podcast that jumps all over the place feels confusing, and people tune out quickly. One of the most valuable skills you will build as you gain experience is the ability to stay focused on your core message without wandering into side stories that do not serve the audience.

This is why planning matters. Before any interview, take a few minutes to outline the main points you want to cover. Write down the ideas you want to hit, the examples you want to use, and the takeaway you want listeners to remember. Even a few notes nearby can help you stay on track.

During the interview, stay centered on a clear theme. Keep your answers tight. Make your point, share a short story if it adds value, and bring it back to the message you want listeners to walk away with. When you stay focused, the conversation feels stronger, the host stays engaged, and the audience gets clear value that reflects well on your brand.

Not Taking Technical Setup Seriously

Many new podcast guests overlook the technical side of things. They mistakenly believe the host will handle it or the editor will clean it up later. That mindset can ruin an otherwise great interview.

Even if a show does light editing, do not rely on someone else to fix preventable problems. If your mic cuts out for ten seconds, the editor might miss it, and that part of your answer is gone for good.

Bad audio can kill your message. If your volume jumps around, your camera freezes, or your mic distorts every time you get excited, people will stop listening no matter how strong your content is. This is why it helps to invest in equipment that delivers a clean, steady sound and to learn the basics of how to use it.

When you record in person and rely on the host's gear, do not assume everything is perfect. Take a minute to run a quick check together. Make sure you can hear yourself clearly. Check that the room is quiet. Pay attention to where the mic is placed. These small details matter more than most people realize.

It also helps to understand a few simple audio and video fixes so you are not stuck if something goes wrong after the recording. Even a basic level of knowledge can save an interview.

Taking your setup seriously shows respect for the host and the audience. More importantly, it protects the quality of your message and helps you deliver an interview you feel confident sharing.

Ignoring Time Constraints

A lot of beginners forget to pay attention to the timing of the show. Every podcast has a general length that listeners expect. If you come in far under that time, the episode can feel thin. If you go far over, people start to drift. Even great content loses its impact when it drags on too long. ,

Before you record, take a minute to check how long the podcast usually runs. Most shows have a rhythm. Some prefer tight fifteen minute interviews. Others run closer to an hour. Knowing that target helps you plan how deep to go with your stories, examples, and tips.

Once you know the general time frame, map out your talking points so everything fits. You do not need a script. Just a simple plan. During the interview, keep an eye on the clock and stay flexible. If time is running short, tighten your answers. If you have extra time, add a quick story or expand a point that deserves more attention. More importantly, it helps you deliver a conversation that feels complete without dragging or rushing.

Forgetting Your CTA or Follow-Ups

Guests will crush the interview and then drop the ball at the very end. They forget to give listeners a clear next step. No CTA, no place to follow up, nothing.

Your CTA does not need to be complicated. Invite listeners to visit your website, join your email list, download a free resource, or check out something useful you created. The key is to keep it simple and make it easy for people to find you.

A strong lead magnet helps as well. It gives listeners a reason to stay in your world and lets you continue the relationship long after the episode ends. Even something small works as long as it offers real value.

Think of the CTA as the bridge between the interview and the start of a longer relationship. When you give clear next steps and have a follow up system ready, you turn listeners into subscribers, leads, or customers. You make it easy for people who enjoyed your message to stay connected with you.

What to Do from Here

Every guest makes mistakes in the beginning. That is part of the process. What matters is that you learn from them and keep improving with each interview. The more you prepare, pay attention to the host, and stay focused on helping the audience, the better your results will be.

If you avoid the common mistakes in this chapter, you put yourself ahead of most beginners. You show up ready. You sound confident. You make the host's job easier. You leave listeners with a clear next step so the relationship does not end when the episode does.

Remember, you do not need to be perfect. You just need to be intentional. Keep refining your message, keep showing up prepared, and keep looking for ways to deliver value. Do that, and you will continue to grow your reach, build your brand, and land more opportunities from every podcast you appear on.

This chapter ends here, but your podcasting journey does not. You are ready for the microphone. Go get booked.

Why This Matters

Podcast guesting rewards intention, not improvisation. The difference between guests who get invited back and those who disappear after one appearance often comes down to small decisions made before, during, and after the interview. Preparation, focus, timing, and follow up shape how hosts remember you and how listeners respond to your message.

When you avoid the mistakes in this chapter, you protect your credibility, respect the audience's time, and make it easier for the right people to take the next step with you. That is how podcast appearances turn into long-term visibility, trust, and opportunity.

Action Step: Prepare Intentionally Before Every Interview

Before your next podcast interview, do the following:

- Research the show's format, tone, and typical episode length
- Write down three core messages you want listeners to remember

- Decide on one clear CTA and where it fits naturally in the conversation
- Do a quick technical check of your audio and video setup
- Set a reminder to follow up with the host after the episode goes live

This takes less than fifteen minutes and dramatically improves how you show up.

You now know what to avoid. In the next chapter, we will pull everything together into a simple guest podcasting game plan you can follow with confidence from booking to follow up.

Bonus Resource: Podcast Guest Readiness Checklist

To help you stay prepared and confident, use this checklist before every interview. It walks you through pre interview prep, key talking points, technical setup, timing awareness, and post interview follow up so nothing falls through the cracks.

Access it here:

seooptimizers.com/bonus

Or scan the QR code below for instant access.

LEVERAGING YOUR GUEST SUCCESS TO LAUNCH YOUR OWN SHOW

Build a platform that grows with you, amplifies your expertise, and turns every conversation into a strategic asset.

"Your brand is what people say about you when you are not in the room."
— Jeff Bezos

Guest podcasting is one of the most effective ways to grow your brand, build authority, and reach new audiences. You step into someone else's established community and connect with listeners who are already open to hearing from you. That alone can transform your visibility and your business.

Hosting your own podcast takes those results even further. It gives you a channel you fully control, where you shape the message, guide the conversation, and build a loyal audience that follows you because they value your insight. This is how my own journey in podcasting began. It led to more interviews, stronger relationships, more clients, and eventually the book you are holding right now.

When I launched my first podcast, there was no big audience and no grand strategy. I recorded simple conversations with people I genuinely wanted to learn from. Each episode made the next conversation easier. Hosts noticed. Guests shared the show. One interview turned into another opportunity, then another. Over time, those conversations created momentum I could never have manufactured with ads or cold outreach alone.

Build Your Own Loyal Audience

Launching a podcast helps you attract listeners who are naturally interested in your niche. They choose you because they want more of your perspective. Over time, this turns into a community that trusts you, follows your content, supports your business, and looks to you for direction.

When you present your ideas in a relatable, interesting, or entertaining way, listeners come back episode after episode. Consistency builds loyalty, and loyalty creates long-term business growth that compounds over time.

Strengthen Your Status as a Trusted Expert

Hosting a show positions you as a credible, reliable voice in your field. Over time, listeners come to see you as someone they can trust, which naturally strengthens your influence and improves conversions across your business.

A podcast also expands your visibility in a way that feels organic. As people share your episodes, reference your ideas, and recommend you to others, your brand grows without constant promotion.

Unlock New Opportunities and Revenue Streams

Your podcast guests turn into warm connections for future collaborations. Listeners who follow your show become warm leads for your offers. Beyond that, you can monetize through sponsorships, partnerships, advertising, and select promotional placements.

Some of my most valuable business relationships did not start with a pitch. They started with a podcast conversation. A guest became a referral partner. A listener reached out after hearing an episode. Several long-term clients first encountered my work through a show I hosted, not a sales page.

Over time, your podcast evolves from a marketing channel into a revenue producing asset that continues to work in the background.

Promote Without Feeling Salesy

One of the biggest advantages of podcasting is how easy it feels to talk about your business. The relaxed, conversational format allows you to share ideas that lead organically into your offers.

When done well, listeners experience it as helpful insight rather than a pitch, which keeps engagement high and protects the integrity of your message.

Stay Current and Connected

Hosting experts and industry leaders on your show keeps you informed and connected to what is happening in your space. You learn through each conversation and stay current on the trends that matter most.

This allows you to evolve, adapt, and remain at the front of your field. A podcast makes ongoing education effortless.

Start Early and Stay Consistent

Anyone can start a podcast. What matters most is showing up consistently. Building an audience takes time, which is why starting sooner allows the benefits to compound over months and years.

Guest podcasting helps you expand outward. Hosting your own show helps you build inward. Together, they create a powerful system. You reach new audiences while growing a community you fully own.

This shift from guest to host is not just a tactical upgrade. It changes how your brand grows over time.

Why This Matters

Guest podcasting helps you borrow attention. Hosting your own podcast helps you build equity.

When you rely only on guest appearances, your visibility is always tied to someone else's platform. When you host a show, you create an asset you control. Every episode strengthens your positioning, deepens trust with your audience, and reinforces your authority long after the recording ends.

This matters because trust compounds. The more consistently people hear your voice, your ideas, and your perspective, the easier it becomes for them to choose you. Not just once, but repeatedly. A podcast allows you to stay present in your market without chasing attention or relying solely on paid promotion.

If you are already guesting on podcasts, you are doing the hardest part. Launching your own show simply gives those efforts a permanent home.

Action Step: Define Your Long-term Platform

Decide whether hosting a podcast belongs in your long-term strategy and take one small step today.

Choose one of the following actions:

- Write a one sentence description of the show you would host, including who it is for and what problem it helps solve
- Create a short list of five people you would want to interview first
- Decide on a realistic publishing schedule you can commit to, even if it is twice a month
- Record a short practice episode on your phone or computer without worrying about publishing it

You do not need a perfect plan. You need momentum. The goal is to move from thinking to doing.

Bonus Resource: Clarify Before You Launch

To help you launch with clarity and intention, use this guide before starting your own podcast. It walks you through defining your ideal listener, clarifying your core theme, selecting the right types of guests, and connecting your show to clear business goals so you build momentum with purpose instead of guessing as you go.

Access it here:

seooptimizers.com/bonus

Or scan the QR code below for instant access.

CONCLUSION: YOUR GUEST PODCASTING GAME PLAN

Let's wrap it up with a clear guest podcasting game plan you can start using today to book more interviews with confidence.

"The path to success is to take massive, determined action."
— Tony Robbins

Throughout this book, we have covered the tools, strategies, and systems you need to turn guest podcasting into a reliable growth channel. These skills apply not only to podcasts, but also to interviews, panels, and any platform where your voice can reach new audiences.

The guest podcasting game plan:

- **Find and Filter**: Build a list of shows that actually move the needle
- **Pitch**: Send value-driven emails that get a yes
- **Prep**: Dial in your tech and messaging
- **Perform**: Deliver value, tell stories, and avoid sounding salesy
- **Promote:** Leverage the content to grow your own authority

When I finally committed to following this exact process consistently, podcasting stopped feeling random and started driving real results.

The Power of Connection

At the heart of this book lies a simple truth. Podcasting is about connection. It is one of the few mediums where you can speak directly into a prospect's ear for 30 to 40 minutes at a time.

In a digital world full of noise and distraction, podcasting allows you to slow down and have a real conversation. It lets you take part in the oldest human tradition of all. Storytelling. By sharing your story authentically, you move from being just another business owner to becoming a trusted voice.

Your Voice Has Value

Many people hold back because they fear rejection. They worry they are not expert enough or that their story is not unique. But the world is full of people who need exactly what you have to teach.

If you stay silent, you miss the chance to help them. When you embrace the challenge and view every interview as an opportunity to serve rather than sell, you begin building a reputation that speaks for you.

Your Next Step

You now have all the tools you need to make the most of every podcast appearance, grow your reach, and expand your authority. Whether you continue guesting, launch your own show, or do both, you are stepping into a higher level of visibility.

Podcasting rewards people who show up consistently and speak with intention. Every conversation becomes part of your digital footprint and your long-term authority. Over time, those conversations shape how people see you, trust you, and choose to work with you.

Start with one pitch or one episode. Stay consistent. Apply what you have learned in this book, and you will create a podcast presence that opens doors, strengthens your brand, and supports your business for years to come.

Step into the conversation, share what you know, and let your voice do the work.

Why This Matters

Guest podcasting is not about chasing attention. It is about building trust at scale. Every interview you do becomes part of your digital footprint.

Long after the episode airs, people will discover you through search, referrals, and recommendations. Those conversations shape how you are perceived, what you are known for, and whether someone chooses to work with you.

When done consistently, guest podcasting compounds. One appearance leads to another. One relationship opens the door to the next. Over time, you build authority that works for you even when you are not actively promoting yourself.

Action Step: Put This Into Practice

The best way to build momentum is to take action while everything is still fresh.

Use the steps below to turn what you have learned into progress this week:

- Identify five podcasts in your industry that align with your audience and expertise
- Draft one value driven pitch using the framework from this book

- Prepare three stories or examples you can share on any interview
- Commit to taking action this week, not someday

Progress comes from consistency, not perfection. One pitch sent today is more powerful than ten ideas that never leave your notebook.

Bonus Resource: Guest Podcasting Implementation Checklist

If you want a simple way to put this into action immediately, I have created a master checklist that covers every step in this book. It walks you through the exact steps to take before, during, and after every appearance so nothing falls through the cracks.

Access it here:

seooptimizers.com/bonus

Or scan the QR code below for instant access.

RESOURCES AND TEMPLATES

Throughout this book, I've shared the exact systems I use to get booked on podcasts, deliver strong interviews, and turn each appearance into long-term visibility, traffic, and leads.

Rather than locking these tools into print, I've made them available online so they can evolve as podcasting, SEO, and marketing change.

Each chapter points you to a specific resource designed to help you take immediate action. Below is a centralized guide so you can easily find what you need when you need it.

Podcast Research and Outreach

These resources support the early stages of guest podcasting, from identifying the right shows to making first contact.

You will find tools to help you:

- Evaluate podcast fit and audience alignment
- Research hosts quickly and efficiently
- Organize outreach and track responses

Pitching and Getting Booked

Strong pitches open doors. These templates help you clearly communicate your value without sounding salesy or generic.

You will find resources to help you:

- Write concise, personalized pitch emails
- Follow up professionally without nagging
- Adapt your pitch for podcast hosts

Interview Preparation and Delivery

Preparation builds confidence. These tools are designed to help you show up calm, clear, and ready to deliver value.

You will find tools to help you:

- Prepare talking points without scripting
- Stay on message during interviews
- Deliver a clear and natural CTA

Promotion and Repurposing

One podcast appearance can fuel weeks of content if you have a system. These resources help you extend the life of every episode.

You will find tools to help you:

- Promote episodes strategically
- Repurpose content across platforms
- Build momentum after each release

Tracking Results and Improving Performance

Guest podcasting works best when you track what matters. These tools help you measure results and refine your approach over time.

You will find tools to help you:

- Track podcast appearances and links
- Measure traffic and SEO impact
- Identify what is working and double down

How to Use These Resources

If you are reading this book cover to cover, use the resource links at the end of each chapter as you go. That is where they will be most useful.

If you are revisiting the book later, use this section as your reference point. Jump straight to tools that match your current goal.

These resources are designed to support action, not overwhelm. You do not need to use everything at once. Start simple, build consistency, and improve with each appearance.

Final Note

Podcasting rewards momentum. The more you pitch, appear, and promote, the easier the process becomes.

This book gives you the strategy. The resources give you the system. Use both, and you will turn guest podcasting into a repeatable growth channel for your brand.

If you want a simple way to put everything in this book into motion, scan the QR code below to access the complete Guest Podcasting Game Plan and supporting templates.

ABOUT THE AUTHOR

Brandon Leibowitz is the founder of SEO Optimizers, a digital marketing agency founded in 2007 and based in Los Angeles. He helps small businesses increase online visibility, website traffic, and qualified leads through SEO, paid advertising, and authority building.

Brandon has been featured as a guest on hundreds of podcasts across marketing, business, and entrepreneurship. On these shows, he shares practical strategies for turning conversations into long-term growth. His guest podcasting framework focuses on building credibility, earning high quality backlinks, and creating content that compounds over time.

When he is not working with clients or recording interviews, Brandon teaches business owners how to leverage guest podcasting as a repeatable system rather than a one off tactic. His approach emphasizes consistency, preparation, and treating every appearance as a long-term asset.

To learn more about Brandon and access resources mentioned throughout this book, visit **seooptimizers.com**

www.ingramcontent.com/pod-product-compliance
Lightning Source LLC
LaVergne TN
LVHW101442200926
848483LV00001B/18
* 9 7 9 8 9 9 4 4 9 3 5 1 9 *